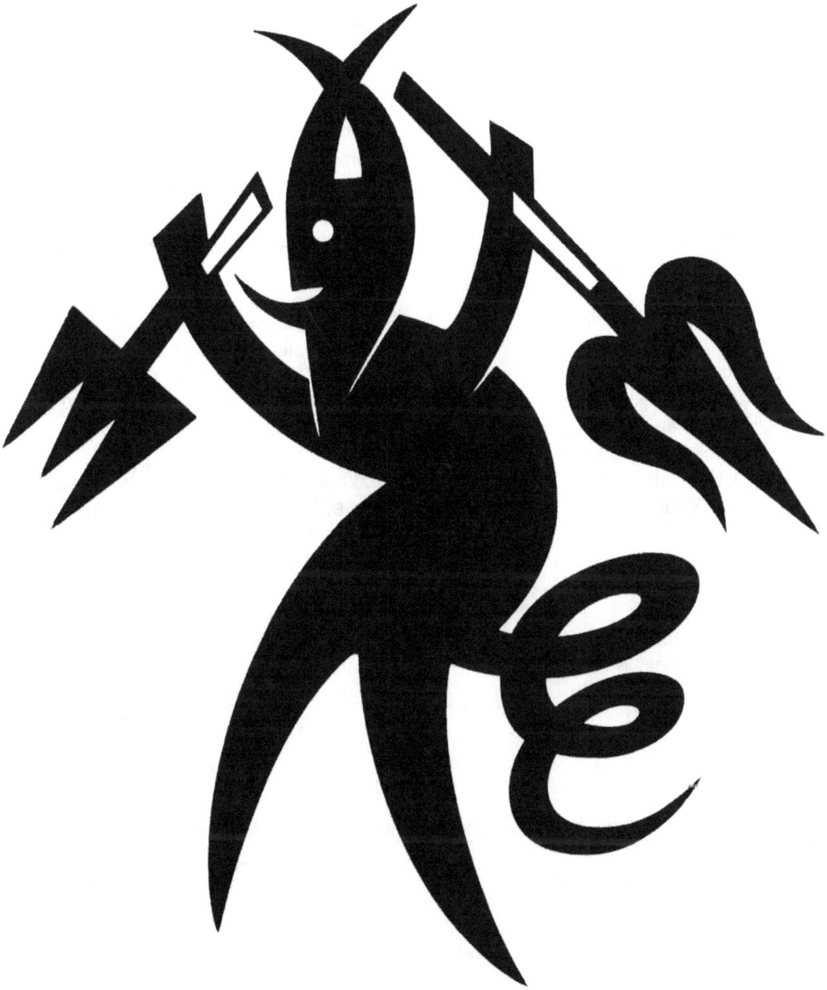

the Reprobate
the final programme

https://reprobatepress.com
email: reprobatepress@gmail.com

www.twitter.com/reprobatepress
www.instagram.com/reprobatepress

Editor / Publisher: David Flint

Writers:
Bruce Barnard, Daniel Black, Gipsie Castiglione, Darius Drewe, Ade Furniss, Hayden Hewitt, Lesley Hopewell-Ash, Daz Lawrence, David McGillivray, Lucy Morrow, Keri O'Shea, Nigel Wingrove

Art and Photography:
Jason Atomic, Gavin Morrow

Acknowledgements:
Satanic Mojo, Trigger Warning, Trunk Records, V&A, Wayne Zenith

Front Cover:
Alexander McQueen / V&A
Back Cover:
Marilyn Chambers, **Behind the Green Door** 1972
Frontispiece: Fortunato Depero, **Tutti all'Inferno!!!** 1922
Editorial:
The Crazies, 1973

All content © 2020 The Reprobate and individual contributors and may not be reproduced without clear written permission from both.

All images are published in the spirit of publicity, and all efforts have been made to contact rights holders. Omissions are unintentional and will be corrected in future editions.

All opinions, ideas, comments and views expressed within the pages of The Reprobate are those of the individual writer and should not be taken as representing the beliefs of the publisher.

All correspondence, in all formats, will be assumed to be for publication, with the writer's name attached, unless the writer explictly states otherwise.

We encourage contributions, but all submissions are sent at the owners risk. We cannot accept responsibility for loss or damage of anything sent to us, or disputes with advertisers - though if you have any, feel free to tell us.

Any naked imagery features consenting adults of 18 years or older.

The Reprobate is a Reprobate Press publication.

Harder... Faster...

discontents

p.4: **Apocalypse Now and Then** *closing arguments*

p.6: **Frank Bough - TV's most unlikely decadent** *from Grandstand to cocaine and bondage parties*

p.8: **In the Blue Ridge Mountains of Virginia** *on the trail of the lonesome pine*

p:11: **Why Do The Beer Censors Think That Women Are Idiots?** *paternalism and condescension for the pregnant*

p.12: **Satanic Mojo Manifesto** *a rallying call for religious liberty*

p.16: **Goat Glands and the Electric Water Conspiracy** *quack cures and bad science*

p.20: **The Hunt for Ugly George** *wither now the Gonzo Porn pioneer?*

p.26: **Twitter Ye Not** *bitesize outrage and the Jack the Ripper Museum*

p.30: **End of Part One** *tv advertising and the way we were*

p.34: **I'm Not defending Rape Porn, But...** *in defence of the indefensible*

p.36: **From the Sacred to the Profane** *sex, scent and sensuality*

p.46: **Death as Art, Art as Death** *the extremes of artistry*

p.50: **Alan Jefferson's Galactic Nightmare** *Spaced out concept rock*

p.52: **Greetings from the Salton Sea** *a trip to a dead resort*

p.64: **Pubic Hair Wars** *to shave or not to shave, that is the question*

p.69: **The Lost Classics of Rock** *Abruptum's Evil Genius*

p.70: **Yes... No... Die!** *the magical myths and tedious truth about ouija boards*

p.74: **Savage Beauty** *rediscovering the art and darkness of Alexander McQueen*

p.82: **Not Now, Mr Cooney** *sex farces of the Seventies*

p.85: **The Lost Classics of Rock** *Don Bradshaw Leather's The Distance Between Us*

p.86: **Behind the Door of the Mitchell Brothers** *porn's hippy pioneers*

p.90: **Violence and Deceit** *the bottom of the British filmmaking barrel*

p.94: **Jordan Peterson vs GQ** *social science meets social justice*

p.98: **Loverboys, Dancing Bears and Partying Hardcore** *Male strippers and horny housewives on the internet*

p.100: **Cancelling Candy** *How Lou Reed's celebration of diversity has been reinterpreted as a hate anthem*

p.102: **Memoirs of a Reprobate** *Remembering the pioneering days of fetish clubbing*

apocalypse now and then
a reprobate editorial

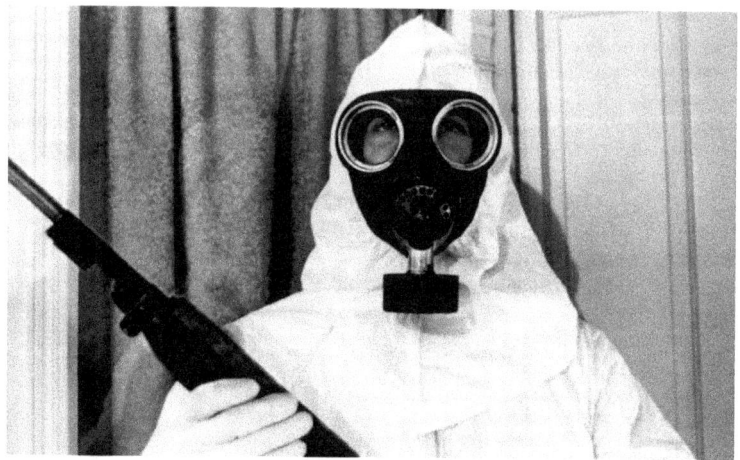

So here we are once more. Welcome to the third and final edition of the **Reprobate** project. Well, when we say 'final', you can never say never, and it's entirely possible that we might do more books under the Reprobate banner – but this is the last in this particular format. The Reprobate Press will now be focusing on individual books, the website and assorted other projects that we hope to get off the ground – indeed, might have already done so by the time that you read this.

This final edition brings together the previously unprinted content of Issue 0, highlights from the two editions of **The Reprobate Times** (which was a fine idea, but unfortunately hampered by personal circumstances) and some stuff that no one has seen before. I think it's a fine collection that nicely sums up what we wanted to do with **The Reprobate** as a magazine, or book, or bookazine – unfortunately, we live in a world of blinkered conformity, and unless you are awash with money, getting a niche project out there is increasingly difficult these days. I never considered **The Reprobate** to be particularly bizarre or incomprehensible, but maybe that's because I'm defiantly weird and obtuse – for the sort of people who run self-consciously edgy bookshops, it proved too much all round. The wrong sort of edgy, I guess.

Of course, we go to press at very strange times. Right now, we are in the midst of a global social lockdown as a new and scary infection rampages across the world, leaving death and destruction in its wake. Whether Covid-19 was the result of grubby Chinese eating habits or escaped from a lab seems almost immaterial now – it's out, it's killing people and it has already changed the world in ways that are hard to comprehend. Where we go from here is the interesting question – you'd hope that, in the face of a real emergency, the identity politics obsessed and the offence culture followers might dial back their obsessions, but at the moment there is a sense of doubling down – perhaps out of desperation. Can the present social justice movement survive this, or is this the beginning of the end, the first step in a cultural shift? Let's wait and see.

What's clear is that we've never quite faced anything like this. Even the name, Covid-19 – chosen because identitarians in the World Health Organisation were terrified that 'Wuhan Flu' or 'Chinese Flu' might be racist – sounds like the terrifying creation of a science fiction novel. It's hard to imagine that the world will come out of this unchanged, but what those changes will be remains a question that no one can answer. All that is certain is that we are balancing on a knife-edge right now – the police in Britain are relishing their new, small-scale police state powers of keeping everyone locked down and indoors a touch too much, and that seems to be the case globally. The public are, by and large, complying with the new restrictions on their movements, but for how long? By the time you read this, we might well have the answers to these questions. Right now, it feels very odd and very unsettling.

One thing that hasn't changed is the insanity of social media – the bubble of self-importance that is only pricked by the odd inconvenient and, for Twitter users, entirely incomprehensible election result. As we go to press, Prime Minister Boris Johnson – and yes, it still feels weird putting those four words together – has emerged from hospital after a battle with the Coronavirus, must to the dismay of the Twitter Left, much of whom were posting comments along the lines of *"I hope he dies"*. This, you might note, from the same people who have been calling for 'kinder, gentler politics' and still call the Tories *"the nasty party"*. Such blindness to your own unpleasantness is hard to comprehend, even when you accept that people are increasingly living in echo chambers that make alternative opinions on pretty much anything beyond belief. These echo chambers don't simply feedback and amplify your own opinions, they also serve to demonise anyone who might think differently – and let's be clear, we're not just talking about huge ideological differences, but minor variations within your own tribe. As someone who finds both sides of the argument rather unpleasant, it's been intriguing to sit back and watch the battles between Radical Feminists and Trans Activists, particularly seeing the former group suddenly coming out as defenders of free speech and complaining about being silenced and monstered, when they have spent years doing exactly the same thing to everyone in the sex industry. It's equally fascinating to see how the social justice movement eats its own, and how no one can be pure enough – time and time again, we see ideologists taken down because they have not kept up with the latest purity tests, or because the movement eventually moves too far even for them.

Similarly, it's fascinating to see the Right position itself as the defender of Free Speech, only to be behave in exactly the same way as the Left whenever someone says the unsayable – if you demand no-platforming, hound people from their jobs and attempt to destroy their lives because they have said something outrageous or even unspeakable (like, say, wishing that someone would die because they are of a different political bent as you), then you lose the right to complain when others do likewise. The Right's adoption of free speech is certainly sincere in some cases, but for others it is a convenient way to critique the increasingly authoritarian Left, and a principle quickly thrown aside when someone has said something that they don't like.

We hope that **The Reprobate** – in print, online, whatever – can be a voice of reason in these increasingly frantic culture wars. We are aware that we might end up being hated by both sides, and that's fine – in a former incarnation, we were publishing magazines that seemed to be loved by extremists on both the Left and Right, and hated by the centre. If we can now be loved by the much-hated Centrists and loathed by the fanatics, that feels like something we can live with.

In the hope that you are one of the people who actually understands and appreciates what we are doing, I'll end with a shameless shout-out for your ongoing support. You can visit our website, you can check out our podcasts and you can support us on Patreon, keeping us going for less than the price of a pint a month. All will be appreciated. And although this is the final Reprobate in this incarnation, rest assured that we are not going anywhere. We have such sights to show you, with a collection of books lined up that – no false modesty here – I believe will be magnificent. Onwards and upwards...

David Flint, April 2020

frank bough - tv's most unlikely decadent

Words: Daniel Black

What makes a true Reprobate? Is it a life lived shamelessly, with every excess and outrage being a public event that only adds to the legend? Or is it maintaining an outwardly respectable façade, seeming to be a pillar of the community and a safe, boring member of the establishment while in fact secretly engaging in eye-watering levels of depravity and spectacularly sordid behaviour?

If the latter, then Frank Bough must count as a reprobate amongst reprobates. Sure, the likes of Oliver Reed would eat him for breakfast when it came to bad behaviour, but we all expected that of Ollie. But Frank Bough? The balding, smiling, woolly-jumpered host of **Grandstand**? The safe pair of hands trusted to launch the BBC's numbingly wholesome **Breakfast Time** in 1983? He seemed the most boringly bland character imaginable. A dull sports presenter turned dull magazine show presenter, and by 1987, the host of the entirely pointless **Holiday** show on BBC1. The very image of respectability, in fact. Conservative with a small (and possibly big) 'C'. The very essence of BBC establishment figures. Interviewed just before the launch of **Breakfast Time**, Bough explained his tedious professionalism, explaining that he would refrain from any alcohol the evening before appearing on TV. To be fair, I doubt if the journalist had thought to ask him about his take on class A drugs and BDSM sessions before work.

So the revelation that when not on TV, Frank Bough was in fact snorting cocaine off prostitutes at wild sex parties, aged 55, came as a real shock to viewers. It was hard enough to even imagine Bough knowing what cocaine and hookers *were*, let along that he was a regular user of both.

In an interview with **The News of the World** – set up in an attempt to limit the damage of a story that they planned to run (I wonder how much coke had been snorted before *that* brilliant decision?), the married Bough revealed that he would attend swingers parties with call girls and

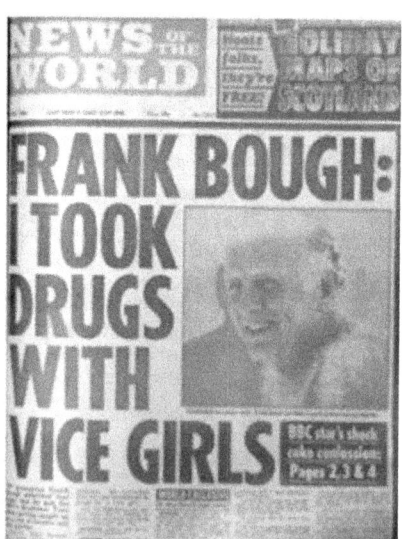

drug dealers, though the drug apparently rendered him incapable of doing anything other than watching couples have sex around him. Oh – and he would often be wearing female lingerie at the time.

He'd apparently been introduced to this world of vice by a French prostitute who he had met at some social gathering or other. *"During the evening, she encouraged me to sniff this white substance which she told me would make me feel better"*, Bough told the **NOTW** (which ran the story on the front page with the headline *"I Took Drugs With Vice Girls"* – so much for damage limitation). *"I can remember seeing three girls and a man fondling one another. There was no question of me joining in."* Lack of participation aside, Bough clearly enjoyed this evening enough to repeat the experience of several occasions.

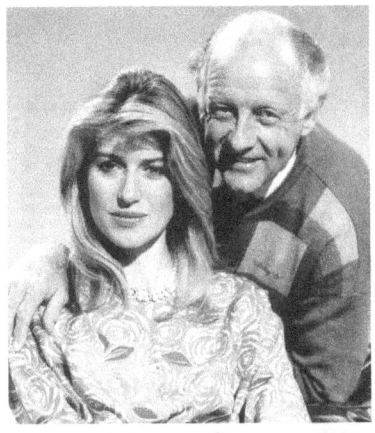

In fact, we would later find out that Bough was quite the character even within the corridors of the BBC, and he clearly had an eye for the ladies. Fellow BBC presenter Fern Britton claims that on one of their first meetings, he said *"well, young lady, I wonder how long it will be before I'm having an affair with you?"*, and would complain that co-host Selina Scott was so frigid that she *"probably rides a bicycle with her legs together"* – presumably, she'd turned down his advances.

These revelations led to Bough being given the boot by an embarrassed BBC, and he spent a few years in the wilderness before being hired by LWT to host their local news show, and then graduated to the ITV network, where he fronted coverage of the 1991 Rugby World Cup. Bough was back, and the viewers were prepared to forgive his previous slip, knowing that Frank had repented. And had this been the one slip, then Bough would hardly qualify as a reprobate at all. Thankfully for everyone, there was more to come.

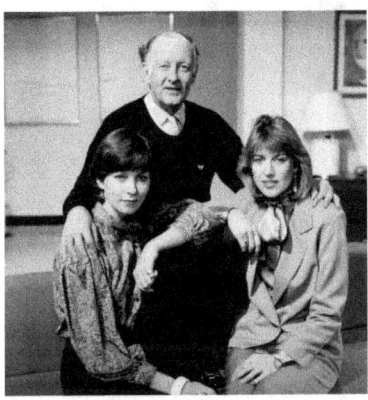

Soon, the press had photographs of him leaving a dominatrix's flat - having been outed by a receptionist at the torture dungeon, where he would allegedly spend up to an hour in a 'torture chamber' – presumably not simply sipping cups of tea and discussing the World Cup prospects for England.

Bough somehow maintained a media career after this second batch of revelations (having undergone the ritual of the televised confession, long-suffering wife by his side, where he expressed *"bitter regrets"* over his actions), though he never hit the dizzying heights of his previous career again.

Long retired – from broadcasting and, I'll assume, reprobating – Bough rarely pops up in the media these days, and it almost – *almost* – seems mean to bring all this up again. But dammit, I'll maintain that Bough was a hero of sorts, striking a rebellious blow against middle aged, middle class conformity and not actually hurting anyone (other than his wife, who stuck with him throughout) in the process. Compared to other BBC presenters of the era, he seems rather wholesome – the figure behind the sort of scandal that I imagine everyone wishes we could have now, rather than the on-going horror stories and childhood memory-shattering revelations that make up the post-Savile era.

in the blue ridge mountains of virginia...

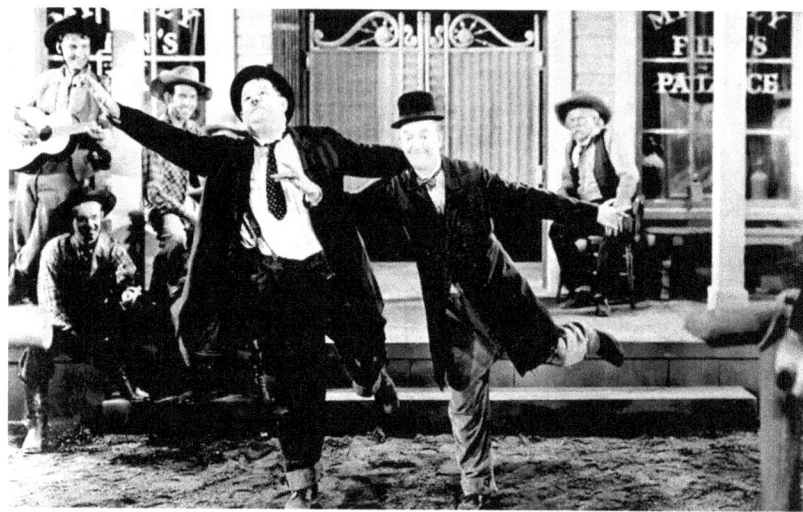

Words: David Flint

In 1937, Laurel and Hardy starred in **Way Out West,** a comedy western that would become one of the duo's best loved films. In common with most comedy films of the era, the movie included a couple of musical numbers, the most famous of which was the 1913 cowboy ballad **On the Trail of the Lonesome Pine** (itself inspired by a 1908 novel of the same name). This plaintive tale of a prospector, lonesome for his girl June, offers a cute interlude in the film – while in a saloon, Stan and Ollie overhear a cowboy (played by Chill Wills) singing the song, and join in. For the first verse and chorus, it's played straight – Oliver Hardy proves to have a pretty decent singing voice – before Stan Laurel takes over, first in a deep baritone, and then, after being hit on the head with a hammer by the peeved Hardy, in a female falsetto. The song ends with Stan passing out. All very entertaining, if not exactly thigh-slappingly hilarious.

Hard as it is for younger people to imagine now, throughout the 1970s and into the first half of the 1980s, you could still see black and white films and TV shows rerun on prime-time TV, without (many) people demanding their colour TV licence being refunded or assuming that their sets were on the blink. Up to 1985 (and maybe beyond), if you tuned into BBC2 around 6pm on a weekday, you could enjoy entire series of Sherlock Holmes or Charlie Chan films, plus Harold Lloyd shorts – and, of course, laurel and Hardy, who were TV staples for decades. Nowadays, with TV schedulers on the public service BBC being as fixated on demographics and ratings as their commercial rivals, such things seem unthinkable.

So I grew up on Laurel and Hardy, and they quickly came to represent the very best of vintage comedy for me. Even as a kid, I was aware that the snooty critics despised Stan 'n' Ollie, finding them too lowbrow, but back then – and still now – I would take them over the plodding, overly sentimental Charlie Chaplin – very much the critic's darling – any day. Laurel and Hardy's mix of slapstick, surrealism, absurdity and careful wordplay seemed to be not only funnier, but a whole lot smarter that Chaplin's little tramp ever could be.

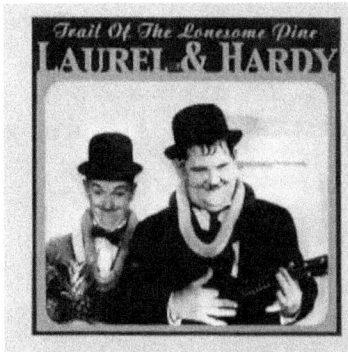

Laurel and Hardy were still enough of a part of the cultural landscape in 1975 for United Artists to release the LP **The Golden Age of Hollywood Comedy**, featuring a mix of songs, music and dialogue from their films. And as was standard practice, the album spawned a single – **On the Trail of the Lonesome Pine**, presented in its original scratchy, lifted-directly-from-the film, monotone glory. Why United Artists felt the need to issue a single is anyone's guess, but it's fair to say that they probably didn't expect a hit – at best hoping for a lower chart placing thanks to the hardcore Laurel and Hardy fans.

Released in late November, the single was picked up by John Peel, then still in his post-hippy, pre-punk phase. Given the climate of the time, it's not as unlikely an event as you might think. A surprising amount of prog rock or the era took a wistful view of the past, and the song wouldn't seem entirely out of place next to Peter Gabriel-era Genesis or other bands fixated on Victoriana and childhood nostalgia – in fact, Vivian Stanshall of the Bonzo Dogs covered the song for Peel, something that makes perfect sense when you listen to his **Sir Henry at Rawlinson End** recordings.

In fact, **On the Trail of the Lonesome Pine** could have almost been made for mid-Seventies radio. Radio One, long before it became desperately youth conscious, loved a novelty hit, especially at Christmas, while Radio Two was firmly in the nostalgic, easy listening market. The song slotted into both sets of playlists surprisingly easily. Still, I doubt very much that anyone quite expected what happened next.

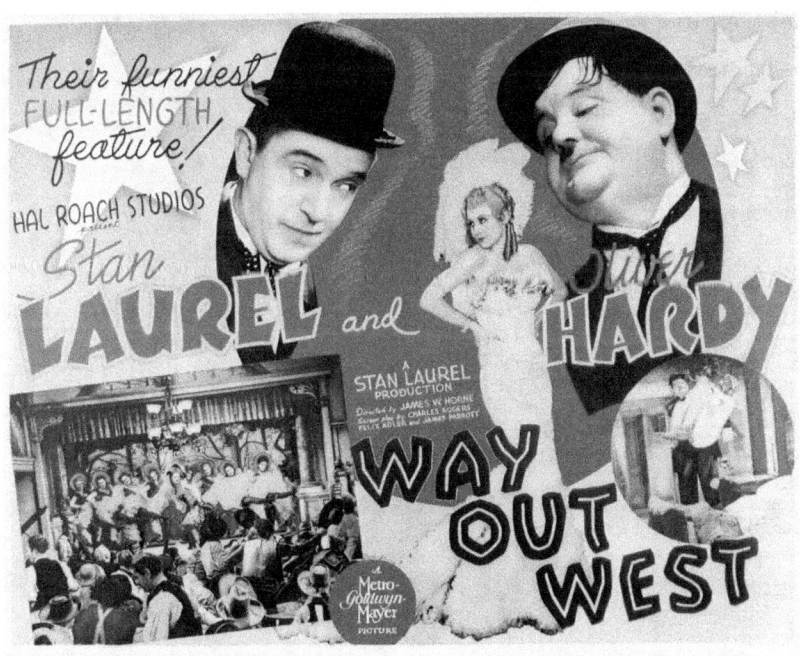

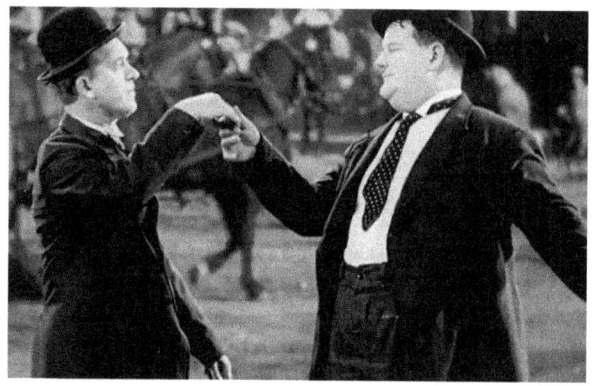

On the Trail of the Lonesome Pine entered the chart at number 48 on the 22nd of November 1975. Outside the all-important top 40, but still a chart placing – I imagine everyone at United Artists was very pleased. But a week later, it had risen to number 21 – quite a jump (again, a note to younger people – once upon a time, it was standard operating procedure for a song to enter the charts in a low position and then steadily climb upwards over a few weeks). On week three, it was at number 9, and by week four, it had reached number three. The record then juggled placed between number three and number two for an astonishing five weeks. It was only kept off the top slot by **Bohemian Rhapsody** (with seasonal numbers like Greg Lake's **I Believe in Father Christmas** sometimes challenging for second place).

The ever-democratic **Top of the Pops** dutifully ran the film clip on a few occasions, and for fans like myself, it was a wonderful time. While I imagine fashionable teens were appalled at such a scratchy old tune outselling the likes of David Bowie, for us kids, it was a song that never got old. Only in the mid 1970s would you find a bunch of short trousered schoolkids knowing the words to an obscure 1913 cowpoke ballad.

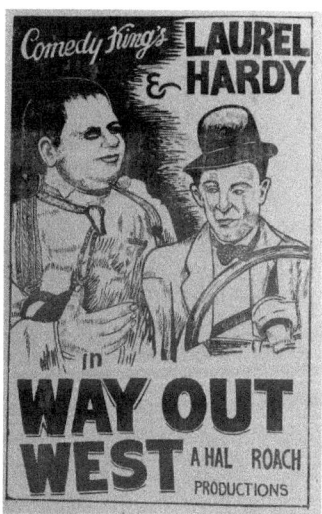

After ten weeks, the song finally slipped out of the top 50. It would later be confirmed as the 39th best selling single of 1975 – not bad, given that it was only available for the last month of that year. Sales figures for the single are hard to come by, but it allegedly sold over £1 million worth of records – and singles in 1975 retailed at under £1, so you can reach your own conclusions at just how much money this record raked in.

We live in too much of a controlled media environment now for something as left-field as this to ever stand a chance of being a hit today. Even in 1975, it was highly unlikely. But wouldn't the world be more fun if songs like this could still be challenging for the number one spot?

why do the beer censors think that women are idiots?

Words: Keri O'Shea

If you're anything like me, then you'll enjoy the odd bottle of beer or cider; likewise, if you're anything like me, then you may have found yourself feeling rather patronised by a certain little logo, which now seems to appear on each and every bottle of booze sold in the country. It's a logo which presents itself as a ban on something, with its recognisable circle around the image and a line through it – though it has absolutely no authority to ban anything. And what does it supposedly veto?

The image in question is a young, pregnant woman, hair scraped into a cheeky ponytail – and a glass of alcohol in her hand, the selfish bitch. Those responsible for labelling our beer want to make it clear in no uncertain terms – drinking in pregnancy is not on. And no consumer, man or woman, young or old, will ever be permitted to forget it.

Thing is, there are a hell of a lot of people who should avoid excessive drinking – if we're going to identify key groups at all. A hell of a lot of people. Here are a few, off the top of my head. Surgeons. Diabetics. People with a history of violence. People with heart disease. People who routinely wield heavy machinery. Stay at home dads. These are all people who might be perfectly fine on a few beers, but may risk their health if they overdo it – but they don't get a logo of their own, and I'm convinced that's not just because it would be a lot bloody harder to design.

The fact is that those joyless cunts at the Portman Group (that most bone-chilling entity, a 'responsibility body') and all of the legislators who willingly roll over for them know that their deep feelings of antipathy towards booze can be best represented with that image. Looking like they only want the best for mums and babies works to their advantage. Because everyone loves babies, don't they? And if we're continually reminded that booze and babies don't mix, with a neat little logo to boot, then the good guy message rumbles on contentedly. We have, after all, created a culture where pregnancy is treated like some sort of exalted state, rather than what it is – a side-effect of contraceptive-free fucking. More than this, pregnancy is a useful political tool, and everyone is all too ready to offer their opinions on 'how best' people should behave. Portman et al know this, and they're using it to their advantage.

The logo, and the message, is as completely redundant as it is dishonest. Of course I'm not advocating women in the family way getting shitfaced – far from it. But there are women who do just that, and it seems unlikely they'll be dissuaded from their actions by spotting the little health warning on their bottle of Lambrini. For the rest of the world's pregnant women, they either already know all of this (in which case the logo is pointless) or else, they know that one glass of wine here or there isn't going to turn Junior into the baby from Eraserhead – in which case, the logo is also pointless. As I say, I'm not advocating pregnant women getting shitfaced. But it seems likely to me that a tiny amount here or there isn't going to make the world spin off its axis. The entirety of Great Britain would have wiped itself out with foetal alcohol syndrome centuries back. Yet it didn't. A glass of stout for a pregnant woman used to come recommended by the doctor. I don't think because we've stopped that practice, we've evolved into higher lifeforms. Could it be that the health risks have been a teensy bit exaggerated for political reasons, and then manipulated by the types of people who either wilfully misunderstand alcohol, or are just too thick to get it? Oh, surely not.

This sort of patronising bollocks is exactly what we have all come to expect, I know. But, in one neat little image, my bottles of beer will now always remind me that the great moral guardians of the British public are out of touch, condescending fucktards. There's a great irony to a 'responsibility body' seeming to think we aren't capable of any responsibility of our own. Especially those silly women.

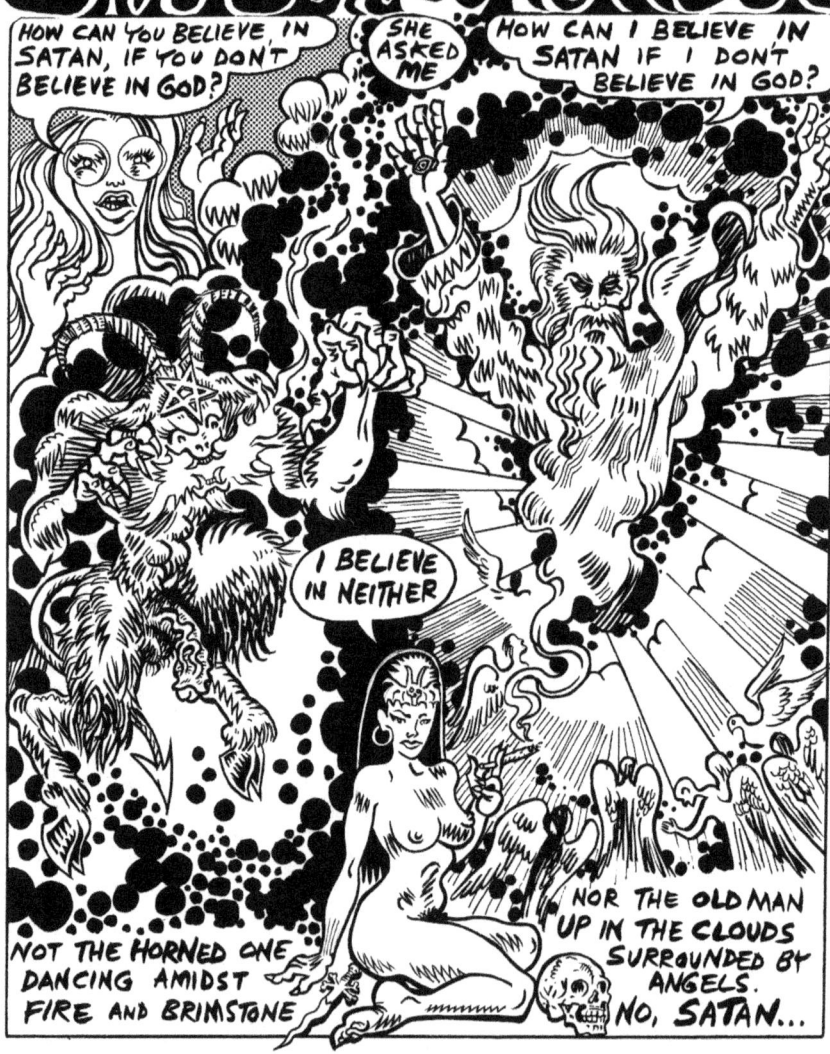

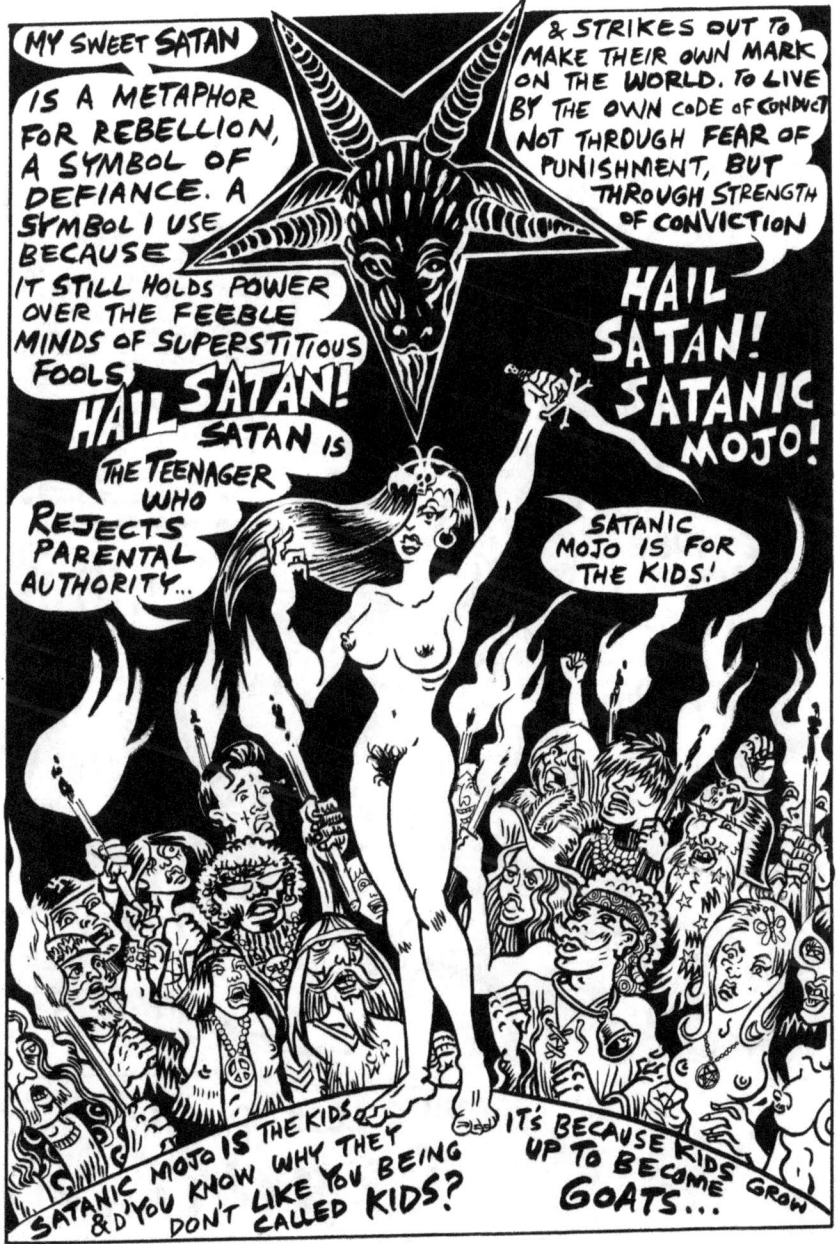

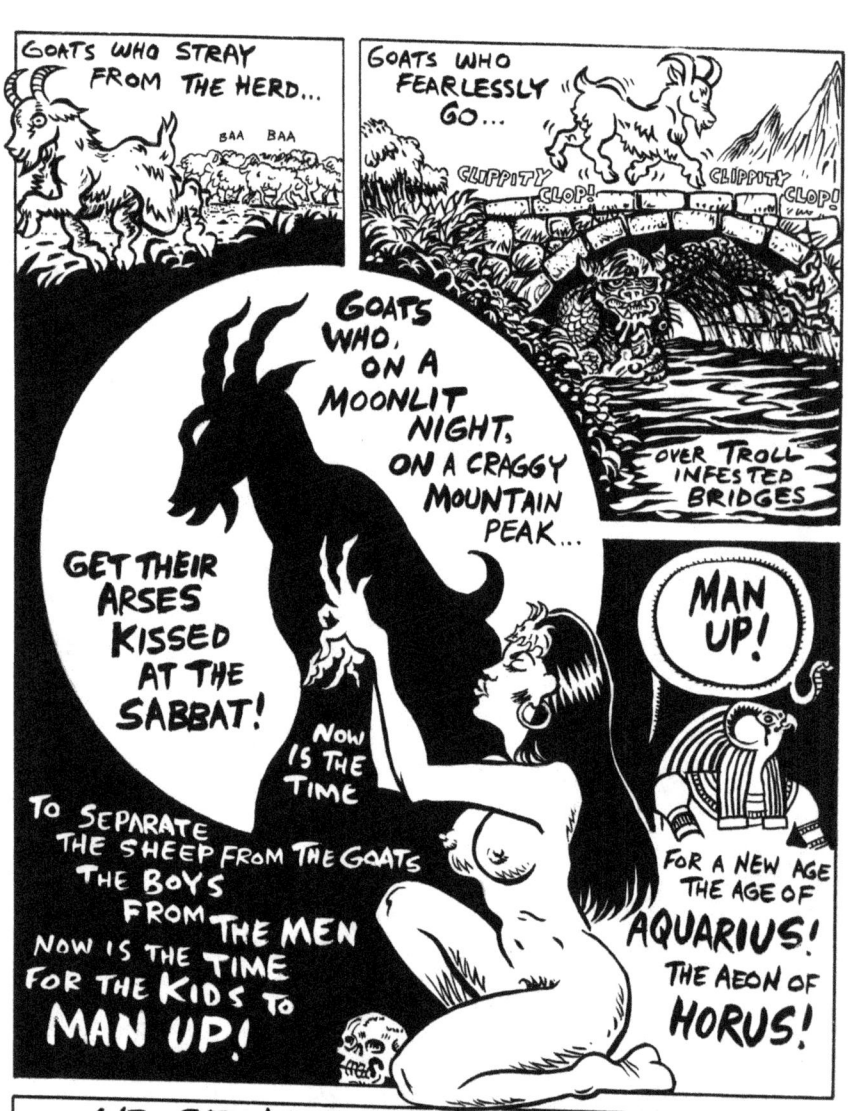

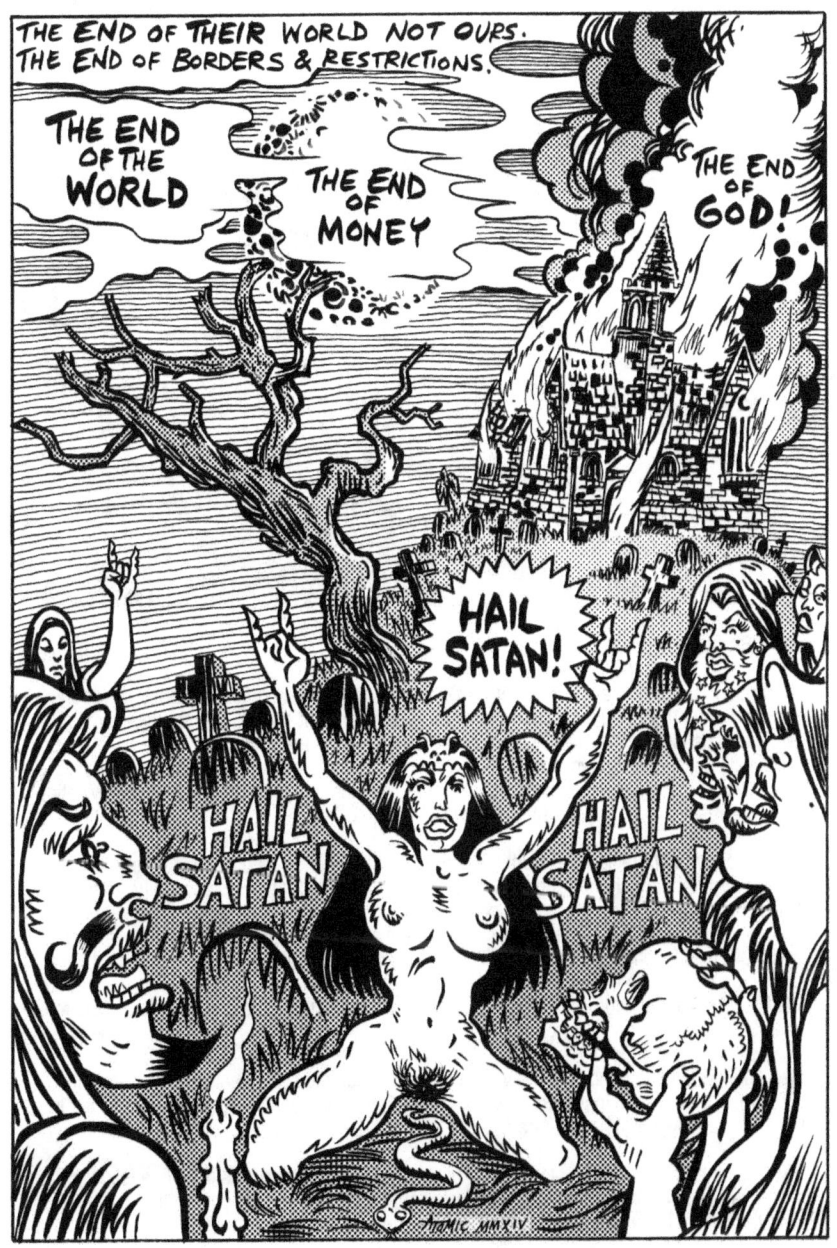

goat glands and the electric water conspiracy

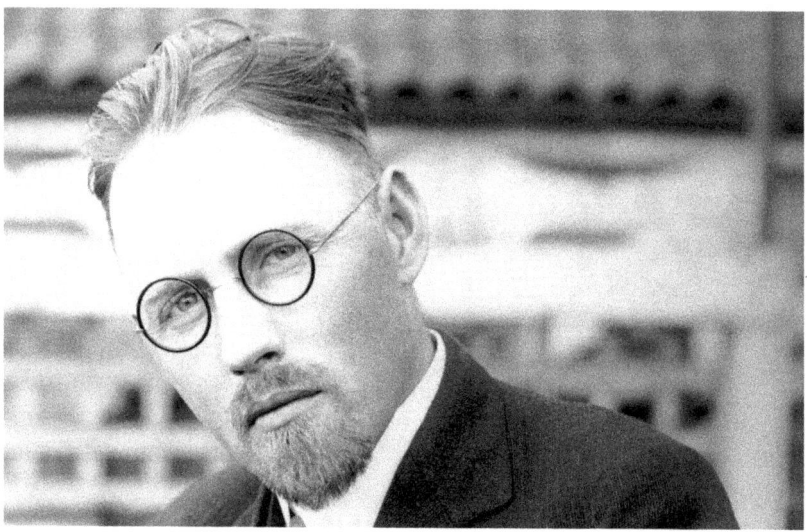

Words: Bruce Barnard

It is March 1915. Just a few weeks before Germany takes warfare into the industrial age by aiming over five thousand cylinders of chlorine gas at Russian troops. The chemicals are designed to cause blindness and ulceration of the throat for any soldier unlucky enough to be caught in the slowly advancing grey fog. If wind conditions are right the results are even more destructive, causing hundreds of dazed soldiers to succumb to choking death by asphyxiation before collapsing into the mud of the trenches.

Meanwhile across the Atlantic, Dr John Romulus Brinkley, failed medical student and bigamist, is fondly remembering the short period he spent singing and dancing as part of the cast of a travelling medicine show. It was during these halcyon days that he made a life changing decision, after coming to the conclusion that there must be a less economically challenging way to fulfil his life long dream of becoming a physician. His ambitions thwarted so far by his inability to fully pay the expensive tuition fees required to complete his studies, he decides to invest $500 for a mail order diploma from a fake university in order to add the initials M.D to his name.

False qualifications in hand he is now licensed to practice medicine in eight Southern US states. After a brief spell in the army, which ends after a nervous breakdown, he becomes free to take any employment he is offered.

He works for a short time at a storefront clinic in South Carolina he sets up with a fellow grifter called Crawford. Their scam is simple and very profitable. The promotion of a new miracle cure which they claim increases 'manly vigour' by the medium of charging hundreds of dollars for a simple injection of tap water luridly coloured with food dye.

The business is a roaring success, not because the placebo works, although there is no doubt the treatment has a psychosomatic effect in some patients, more as a direct result of Brinkley's aggressive advertising campaign. An expensive PR exercise that uses direct mail shots, street level carnival barkers and acres of newspaper print to alert the public to his medical miracle .

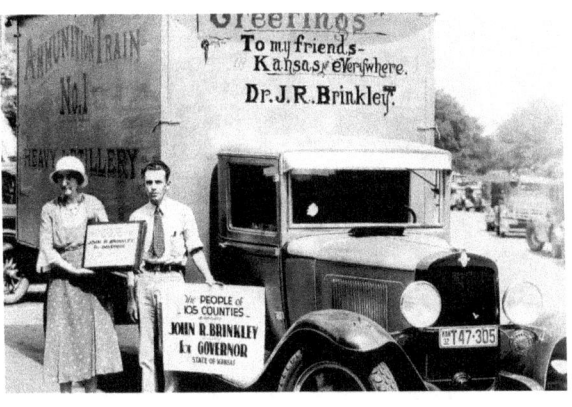

The duo chose to promote the faux treatment as German 'electric water' in order to add an aura of European cosmopolitan mystique. Within days of setting up shop they are swamped by men crippled with shame as a result of their sexual dysfunction, often working long hours in order to treat the queues which stretch along the high street. It also helps that Brinkley is described by those who know him as the very definition of a charming Southern gentleman. One of his patients saying, *"he could charm a wagon out of a ditch"* in reference to the good doctor's bed side manner.

In what would become something of a reoccurring theme in the life of the ambitious Colonel Sanders look-a-like, the business eventually closes down because the pair fail to pay their outstanding bills. As word spreads of their financial incompetence and angry debtors gather to discuss a plan of action, Brinkley and Crawford pack up their snake oil and leave for pastures new.

Soon Brinkley finds work as a staff doctor at a Kansas meat packing company. This a tedious job that mostly involves stitching the wounds of workers whose choice of career involves the risks inherent in using razor sharp knives on a fast moving production line. Bored and irritable he has to find ways to make the hours pass and devotes himself to the study of animal physiology to pass the time, becoming increasingly obsessed with the mating habits of the livestock kept at the plant. Specifically, the keen enthusiasm shown for coitus within the large population of goats awaiting butchering.

The radical idea that will make his fortune comes as a result of a casual conversation with a local farmer, Bill Stittsworth, who brings in his fattened livestock for slaughter to the plant. Whilst discussing the weather, Bill candidly expresses some frustration at a problem that has recently been haunting his marital relations.

"I've got no lead in my pencil, no powder in my pistol", he says.

In a moment of divine inspiration the good doctors mind quickly visualises the raw libido of the rampant bucks in his care and comes to a simple, if somewhat radical, conclusion:

"You'd have no problems if you had a pair of those goat glands in you", he remarks.

Rather than recoil in revulsion at the prospect of a clinical procedure more suited to the House of Pain in H.G. Wells **Island of Dr Moreau** than surgery in any traditional

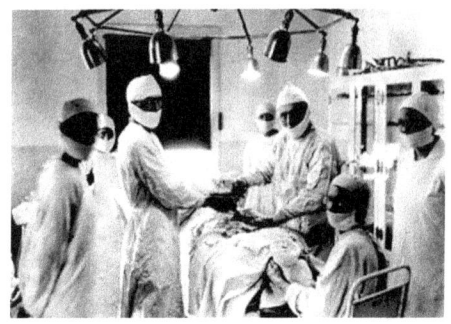

sense, Brinkley claims that Sittsworth begs him to perform the surgery as soon as possible. A statement his son denies in later years, claiming that his father was offered a large sum of money as motivation for acting as a human guinea pig. Whatever form the deal takes, we do know that an appointment is booked and Brinkley sets himself the task of preparing for his surgical debut.

The operation itself is relatively simple, even for a man of Brinkley's limited medical training. After scrubbing up and delivering basic anaesthesia to the patient, thin slices of flesh are extracted from the testicles of a recently slaughtered goat and are inserted into the patient' scrotal sac following a small incision.

Although quick, the procedure has a number of serious flaws, not least the refusal of the host body to accept the foreign tissue, which often leads to infection and necrosis at the suture site. Also complicating matters is Brinkley's habit of performing surgery after having a few robust snifters to steady his nerves. A habit that causes to him become the subject of frequent litigation over the years. Although always reluctant to vocalise any problems with his treatments, Brinkley will occasionally admit, if pushed, that the insertion of the goat testes can make patients ooze a strong animal musk, making them *"reek like a steamy barn in mid-summer"*.

Buoyed by the success of his botched debut (in the sense that the patient had survived the surgery if nothing else), Brinkley soon sets up a state of the art sixteen bed clinic in order to dramatically increase the number of daily operations he can perform. The goats are kept penned in outside the back door, allowing potential clients to hand pick the animal of their choice before being taken to the operating theatre.

Surprisingly Brinkley's investment pays off as a result of a medical fluke, Stittsworth's wife becoming pregnant just weeks after the operation. An event that Brinkley is quick to capitalise on, taking out

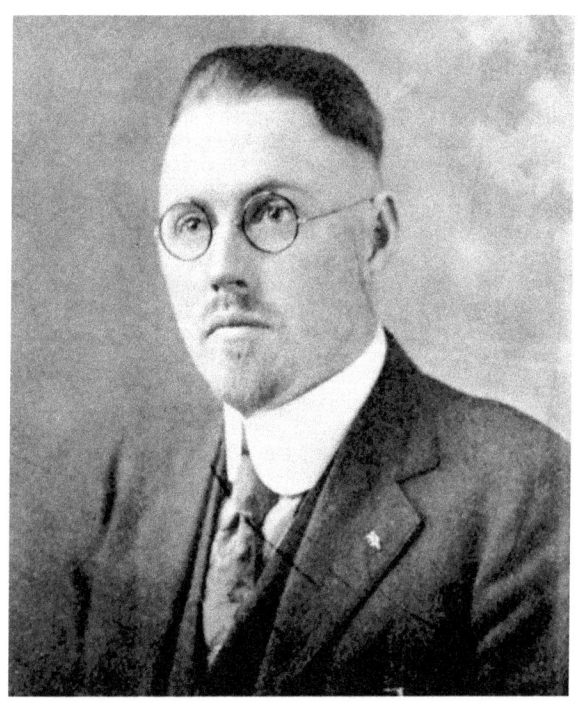

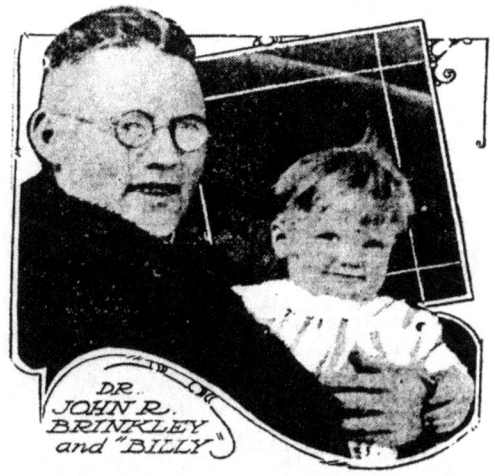

HE'S FIRST GOAT-GLAND BABY

DR. JOHN R. BRINKLEY and "BILLY"

acres of newspaper advertising proclaiming the sexual benefits of his miracle cure. As a marketing strategy it brings in hundreds of clients, but also alerts his repulsed medical peers to his unique brand of dangerous quackery.

Charging $750 per operation means that Brinkley quickly becomes incredibly wealthy and invests further in spreading news nationwide about his discovery. At one stage he even starts his own radio station promoting his operations in-between musical interludes and comedy sketches. The only dark cloud on the horizon is the hundreds of malpractice cases awaiting his attention in court and an ongoing investigation by the American Medical Association. The group forced into taking action when rumours reach them of a macabre twist in events, when Brinkley starts touting a new procedure available for $5,000, where instead of goat testes he will use flesh from the glands of recently hung death row inmates, these secretly sourced from a sympathetic prison warden over the border.

"War Is a racket", declared retired Major General Smedley Butler, in reference to how big business benefits from armed conflict. His iconoclastic outlook evidenced by the profits made at the time by Beyer, the German pharmaceutical giant which supplied the chemicals required for production of the poison gas used in the 1915 attack on Russian troops.

Whilst Brinkley would eventually die penniless in 1938 as a result of legal action and continuing litigation aimed at methods described as 'immoral', the power of capitalism dictated that Beyer would go from strength to strength. In fact their profits increased dramatically throughout World War II, mostly as a result of their production of Zyklon-B, the genocide agent used in the Nazi death camps.

Fast forward into time to just under a century later, where Brinkley's methods are now the subject of much ironic laughter and his position of charlatan is set into cultural stone. In direct contrast we find Beyer's profits going through the roof. This mostly a result of a new miracle cure for erectile dysfunction called Levitra, aggressively marketed as an alternative to market leader Viagra.

One hopes that on hearing this Brinkley would be laughing, rather than turning in his grave.

the hunt for ugly george

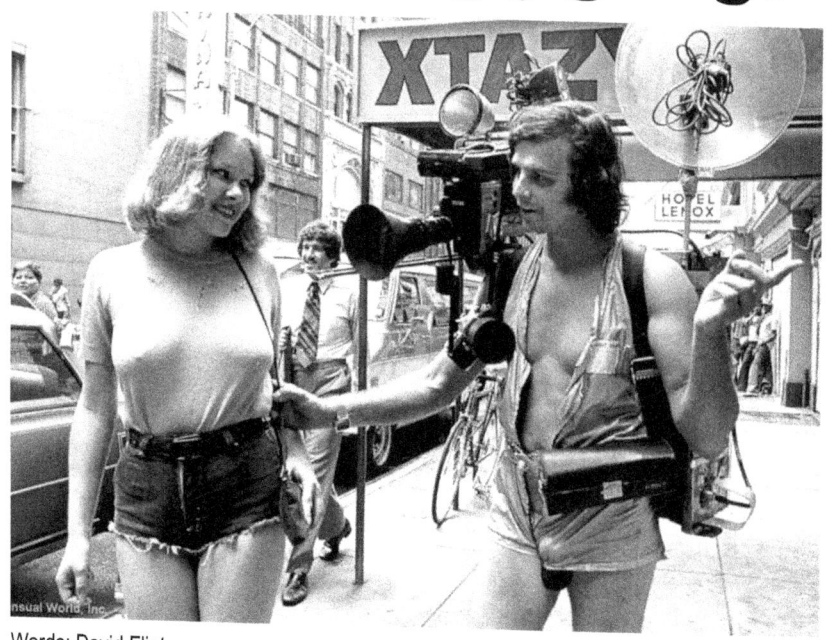

Words: David Flint

"This programme is not to be viewed by children, as it contains nudity and some serious discussion on sexual values in our great nation. It is not a production of the cable company, who are not responsible for its content. If you do not wish to see a programme containing nudity, then turn to another channel immediately, but do not deprive others of their constitutional right to view a programme of their choice. Tuesdays, Wednesdays, Thursdays at 11.30."

I first discovered Ugly George in the early hours of November 5th, 1980. In their wisdom, the ITV network in Britain decided that the best way to cover the unfolding US Presidential election of that year was to offer an all-night collection of the weirdest examples of American public access cable TV that they could find, under the title **The All American All Night Show**. This was a fairly unique idea – British TV's three channels still tended to close down by midnight in those days. The frequently-broadcast trails for the extravaganza predictably emphasised the bizarre and the salacious with typically British hypocrisy (sneering at the bad taste of Americans while using it to pull in viewers), and newspaper reports eagerly hyped the fact that the show would include footage of - shock! Horror! - NAKED CHAT SHOWS!

And while nudity was far from a rare sight on British TV in the 1970s, this was something else – sex for the sake of sex, apparently unhampered by context or artistic validity. As a thirteen year old already obsessed with the bizarre – and still several months away from having a VCR in the house – this was irresistible stuff, and although I'd have to be up for school in the morning, I was determined to sit up all night for this extravaganza of trash. You can do that sort of thing when you're a horny teenager.

Somewhat predictably, the show itself was a pretty shoddy mish-mash. The oddball, demented and trashy moments were invariably scattered among longer, often worthy clips that tested my resolve (I have a vague memory of a lengthy piece about homeless people that may well have been socially important, but felt heavy going at 4am when I was hungry for tits). Intercut with all this were regular updates on how the election was going. Equally predictably, the stuff everyone had tuned in to see – the sexy bits – were kept until the end. But at around 5.30 in the morning, there it was. The nude chat show turned out to be pretty dull, even then – I seem to recall blurry footage of generally unattractive fat people sitting around, naked and bored looking, before doing something that may or may not have been sexual – between the poor quality camerawork and my black and white portable TV, it was hard to tell. After several hours of viewing, this would have been crushingly disappointing had it been the entirety of the naughtiness. But in fact, it was okay, because we also saw clips from **The Ugly George Hour of Truth, Sex and Violence**.

Ugly George (real name George Urban) was a cable TV phenomenon. Walking the streets of New York, dressed like a down-on-his-luck extra from a really cheap sci-fi movie (or perhaps a low-rent escapee from Studio 54) in a silver lamé outfit and lugging a huge video camera, satellite dish and God knows how much more equipment – designed to give him hands-free access and not have to use a viewfinder - about with him, George would approach young women (or *"goils"*) and sweet talk / brow beat them into accompanying him back to some grotty apartment, corridor or alleyway (or, to use his own words, *'"dimly lit hallways"*), where they would strip with varying degrees of enthusiasm, sometimes accompanied by George himself as he came out with a string of self-deprecating comments while he dropped his pants and felt up the hapless gal . George's show happily showed his successes and his failures (the latter ranging from girls laughing in his face to giving him a mouthful of abuse), his strange celebrity encounters and his general meanderings. It was entirely, utterly unique. And the few moments shown to me in those early hours had a major impact.

Over the next few years, clips from **Ugly George** would occasionally turn up on TV – usually in shows hosted by the likes of Clive James or Chris Tarrant that laughed at the terrible, trashy TV that the rest of the world broadcast (while again using said terrible TV to boost ratings). He also turned up in anti-porn polemic **Rate It X** in 1986, where he was naturally portrayed as a predatory monster.

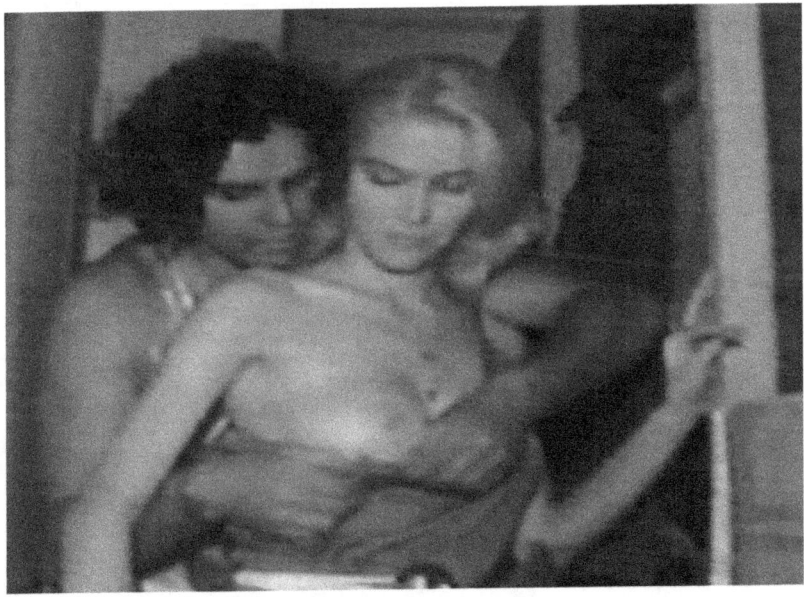

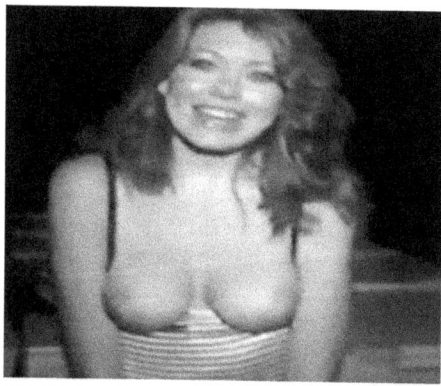

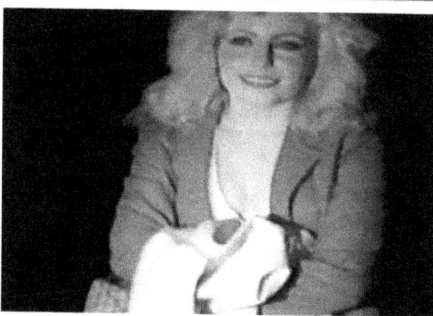

The more I saw – brief, tantalising moments – the more intrigued I became. By this time, I'd seen plenty of actual, no-nonsense hardcore porn on video, but Ugly George was different. His work seemed more honest, more *real*. I needed to see more.

But doing so was almost impossible for a teenager in Northern Britain. Mary Whitehouse might have condemned the newly-born Channel Four as the home of smut peddlers, but they were hardly going to start importing this show – the best we got was 'risque' Canadian sketch show **Bizarre**, which ITV gave a run in the early Eighties and - gratuitous boob shots or not - it was hardly the same. British softcore video magazine series **Electric Blue** seemed to have the answer when they released a compilation tape, imaginatively called **Ugly George.** But **Electric Blue** had fallen foul of Manchester's evangelical Chief Constable James Anderton, who issued a fatwa against the strand – enough to put most video rental shops off stocking the series.

Then came the Video Recordings Act, and the tape was pulled from sale until it was finally approved by the BBFC in 1989 – ludicrously (even for the time) rated R18, which restricted its sale to licensed sex. There were few licensed sex shops around back then, and most of them didn't sell **Electric Blue** titles, so in reality, the availability of the tape was pretty much restricted to **EB**'s own Kings Cross store, where a tape would cost forty or fifty quid. And by the early 1990s, both the **Electric Blue** label and their shop were confined to the dustbin of history.

But by 1989, the influence of Ugly George had begun to seep out into the porn mainstream. John Stagliano shot his first Buttman film - **The Adventures of Buttman** - that year, effectively giving birth to the 'reality' (actually staged, but with a first person 'chat up' technique very similar to George's work) genre of 'Gonzo Porn' (the same year saw the launch of the pseudo-amateur **Dirty Debutante** series and the notorious pick-up **On The Prowl** tapes – all three titles starring the late, great Jamie Gillis, interestingly). The Reality approach that George pioneered rapidly became a major part of the adult industry – the biggest part these days, where wall-to-wall Gonzo sex and pro-am productions dominate, thanks to the proliferation of tube sites and the associated decline of narrative-based hardcore. But George - the inventor of the genre - seemed missing in action.

Certainly, he no longer commanded airtime on British TV. Channel Four's Friday night forerunner to **Eurotrash** was **Manhattan Cable**, a weekly show that – like **The All American All Night Show** back in 1980 – sought out the weirdest of US cable TV, mixing the eccentrics and the lunatics with just enough T&A to keep post-pub viewers watching. But none of that T&A came via Ugly George. And he was just as absent from the **Manhattan Cable** VHS bootleg that circulated in the early 90s – no relation to the show, this consisted mostly of hilariously lurid sex phone line ads (976-PISS, anyone?) interspersed with naked chat shows that seemed even less erotic than their 1980 predecessor had.

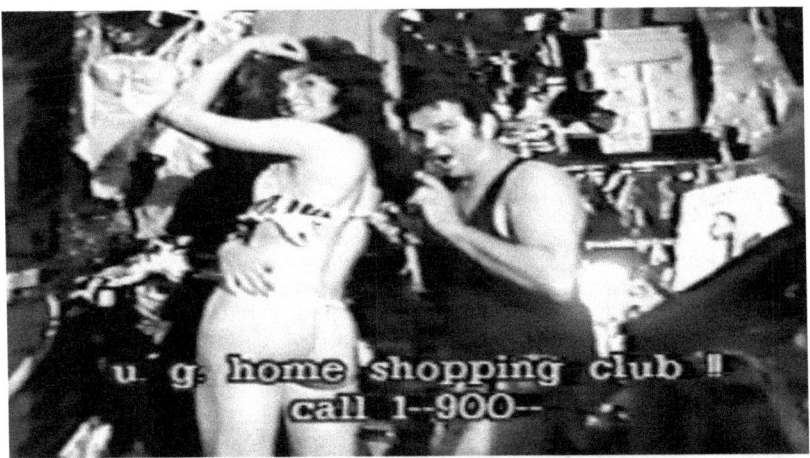

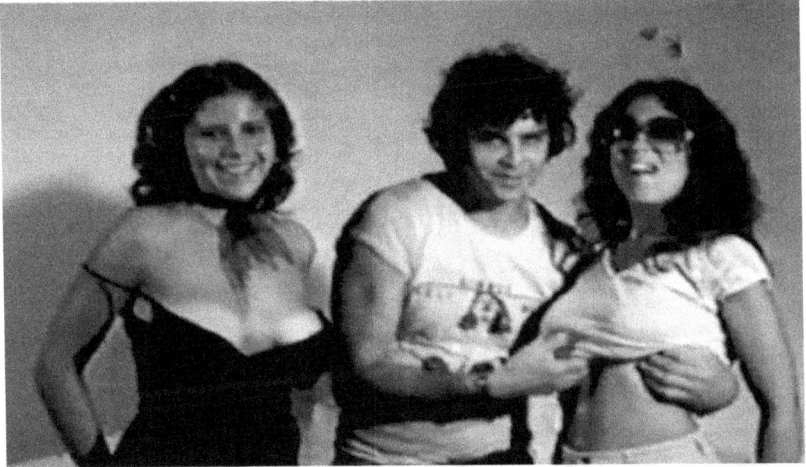

An Ugly George tape did appear on the bootleg circuit – not the **Electric Blue** compilation, which seemed to have vanished without trace, but some horror called **The Big Busted Girls of Ugly George,** which consisted of badly shot video footage featuring generally unappealing – though certainly busty – women stripping and awkwardly trying to look sexy. It didn't have any of the appeal of the Ugly George clips I remembered. In fact, it was so awful, I began to wonder if my memory was playing tricks on me. Had Ugly George actually been that interesting? Or had my adolescent arousal blinded me to his dreadfulness?

In the absence of any video evidence, it was impossible to know. And so another decade passed. But the internet eventually provided *some* answers – though not many. Ugly George might not have been entirely erased from the history books, but he's barely acknowledged – there isn't even a Wikipedia page about him. After some searching, I discovered that George began broadcasting in 1976 and went off-air in 1982 – or was it the early Nineties? It's all a little vague. But some stories are consistent - disagreements with the cable company saw him yanked from the airwaves five times before the plug was finally, permanently pulled. I read that he was planning a comeback in 1998... and again in 2004. Photos of a fatter, greyer, uglier George appeared – the same suit, the same equipment now held together by duct tape and looking as shabby and out of date as its owner – groping porn stars at what looks like a adult entertainment convention. His street activities seemed restricted to photo ops. I visited his website, a bizarre mess combining a handful of photos, incomplete press clippings and entirely unrelated links with possibly the worst web design I've *ever* seen. Amongst the chaos, there is mention of a video club, but as the site hadn't been updated since 2006, I was reluctant to send any money. And now, the website seems to have completely vanished.

Then, I found that there is a documentary about George. Hallelujah! **Boob Tube: Sex, TV and Ugly George**, made in 2007, is not listed on IMDb, but Amazon stocked it – though they never actually had any copies available, and it now seems to have been removed from their inventory. The trailer is on YouTube, and looked interesting, but an attempt to visit the production company website set off all the alarms on my browser, warning me that it is a malicious site that will damage my computer, steal my identity and probably murder my family. This hardly seems a good way to promote your film production, so I assume they've been infected and haven't fixed it – which again, hardly makes me confident about sending them any money.

But thanks to the wonders of the internet, a copy recently came my way. But while it might fill in some gaps about Ugly George's history, reveal him to be a rather sad, angry, egotistical and probably somewhat unbalanced person and pontificate on his influence (they cite **Girls Gone Wild** as a descendent, which I guess is true), I still can't satisfy my curiosity, because all it features from the George oeuvre are the same tantalising clips. I need more. I need it *all*. Finding this documentary is just a reminder to me that I'll probably never get it, because it all seems to be lost. It might still exist on off-air recordings hidden away in basements, but that's it. The bulk of Ugly George's work seems lost forever.

But strange things happen, and sometimes, good things *do* come to those who wait. At the end of 2010, my long quest came to an end – sort of. I found someone who not only had the **Electric Blue** tape, but also some extra Ugly George material – and he was happy to burn it all onto a DVD for me.

Holding the disc in my hand, I wondered if I *should* watch it? How could it possibly live up to almost three decades of anticipation? But I realised that it didn't matter. It *had* to be seen. How good or bad it was hardly mattered anymore – the sense of closure that it would bring was reward enough.

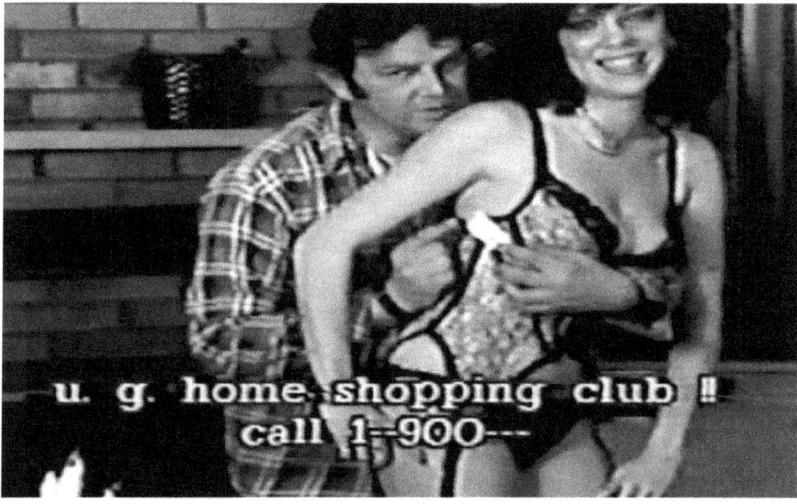

So how was it?

Well, perhaps inevitably, the DVD didn't provide the final chapter to the story. **Electric Blue**'s VHS compilation is a random, choppy selection of clips – a good sampler perhaps, but throwing too much into the 50 minute running time. What's notable is that the girls are a mix of reasonably pretty and fresh faced, and somewhat homely (to be polite), and the whole thing has a curious air of innocence about it – the fact that this harmless effort was restricted to sex shops in the UK is a sad reflection on just how bad our censorship used to be. If nothing else, the video is a curious artefact of a lost world – a New York before Times Square was cleaned up and 42nd Street was stripped of the grindhouses, peep shows, porno theatres and sex establishments, and where a man in a dodgy silver outfit toting a satellite dish could wander the streets propositioning young women without being arrested. There's something quite sweet about it.

That's not a word that can be used to describe the remaining content. Another compilation of unknown origin, this might more accurately reflect the Ugly George show – continual ads for premium rate phone services, sloppy editing and little actual content. George is older in some sequences – already looking like a sad parody of himself. Depressingly, several clips are the same as those seen in the **Electric Blue** tape – surely with at least six years worth of broadcasts, there must be a *few* more clips available? Or perhaps there aren't - it seems that he, like the BBC, wiped huge chunks of his archives, or lost it during periods of homelessness The lengthiest piece strays briefly into hardcore territory, with a young woman giving him a somewhat unenthusiastic blowjob before he attempts to have sex with her (it's unclear exactly how successful he is in his efforts). It's undoubtedly honest – no one would stage-manage anything so utterly, pathetically unerotic – but unlike the earlier footage, this clip is utterly crass and charmless.

So, what have I learned about Ugly George after thirty years of curiosity? That he was a pioneer, certainly; that he failed to move with the times and capitalize on his infamy, probably. There are still unanswered questions, and obsessive that I am, I won't be *really* satisfied until I've seen *all* his material, and that is unlikely to ever happen.

Ugly George both was of his time and ahead of his time. In a porn industry dominated by Gonzo producers and director, many of whom weren't even born when George was at the height of his fame, he's little more that a footnote in history, if remembered at all. As a forerunner of pretty much everything the industry is doing these days, he deserves better – but as with most ageing rock bands, any thoughts he might have of reliving the glory days are probably best ignored.

twitter ye not
bitesize outrage and the jack the ripper museum

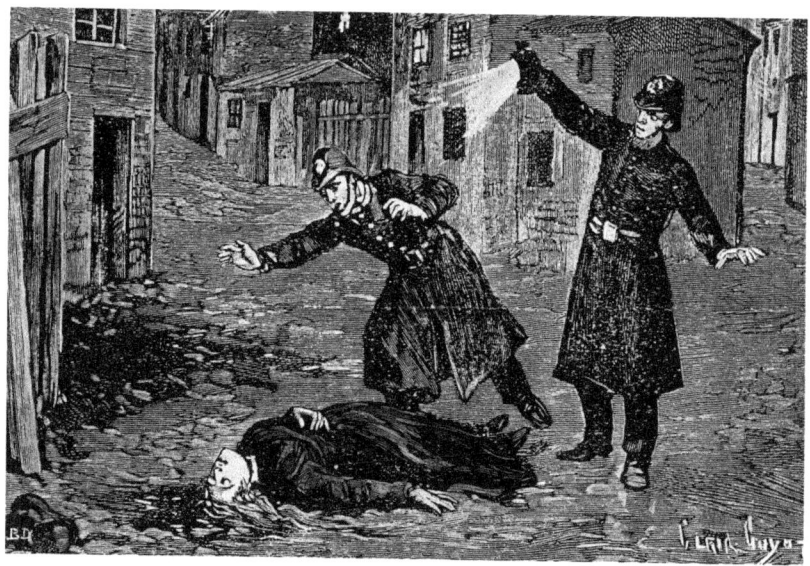

Words: Keri O'Shea

I've seen outrage-hobbyists get bent out of many things on social media over the past few years, but this week was a first. Never until this week had I seen people protesting about a plastic whistle.

I'd made the mistake of assuming that the shitstorm surrounding the new Jack the Ripper Museum on Cable Street had died down and that the small band of protesters so furiously vocal in its opposition had, presumably, been made to return to whatever it is that pays their bills. Not so, if Whistlegate is anything to go by – and what's more, if a furore can be stirred up by a photo of a whistle, then it makes the protests by the same people who recently enjoyed throwing paint at a cereal cafe far more ominous (as someone commented earlier this week, you don't take paint to a protest expecting to take it home).

Before I deal with them, though, I must come back to the whistle, because despite being nothing more than an unfortunate piece of museum gift shop tat, it has now come to speak volumes about the people who want this museum shut down because it doesn't suit their own warped, ever-narrowing channel of ideas on what constitutes 'right' and 'wrong', 'good' and 'bad'.

The protesting women – and their white knights – are in part in such high dander because they believe the JTR museum reduces women to victims, to nothing more than, as has been described, a 'red smudge', as per the museum's logo. However, the same cohort can look at a whistle and see a 'rape whistle', can turn a fairly innocuous naff souvenir into an emblem of... victimhood, sexual violence and fearfulness. With no irony whatsoever, mind, so far as I can tell.

Needless to say I don't follow this thinking, and I'm pretty perplexed by it, all told. If I was going to associate a JTR whistle with anything at all, then it would be with the Peelers who policed the streets in the Victorian era, and beyond that – very little, actually. Shopping for a makeshift rape alarm in a gift shop would be furthest from my mind and, if I was a betting woman, I'd wager the same could be said for whoever green-lit the whistle to be shelved alongside the rest of the pencil sharpeners, mugs and novelty notepads in said boutique.

Those who believe the item in question has any relevance or relationship to rape, well, that worries me. Either these people have deliberately worked themselves up into a lather about nothing at all purely to reinvigorate a sorry, manageable little cause, or else – more worryingly – there are people out there who genuinely believe that the world is so terrifying and awful that a chance purchase = safety system.

Whistlegate is one thing. However, there's more to the rationale behind the actions of the anti-JTRM cabal – that Just Cause which drives them on – and in a nutshell this is that they're terribly upset, because the Cable Street premises were originally earmarked as a Women's Museum. Currently, their demand is not that the JTRM gets 'shut down', simply that it changes drastically to suit them (so – shuts down, then) in order to become 'a celebration of the lives of the women of the East End'. One could argue that striving to contain hundreds of years of female history into one small museum would be impossible, or it may be too broad, or indeed that any depictions of the fates of, say, the East End women who developed 'Phossy jaw' would be just as grisly as anything the existing museum has to offer; for whatever reason though, the lofty, barely-formed notions of the preferable enterprise didn't come to be, and the JTRM moved in instead.

In so doing, it has become just a small part of a fascination which has spawned an industry; in fact, you'd think that any outrage now about Saucy Jack would be a bit late in the day, considering the sheer amount of books, articles, blogs, fiction, film and TV which has been spawned by the Ripper murders (and many of those arguing against the JTRM seem pretty well-versed in the details of the murders themselves, and so at some stage have readily partaken of this industry). The fact that the new museum is small, new and vulnerable is

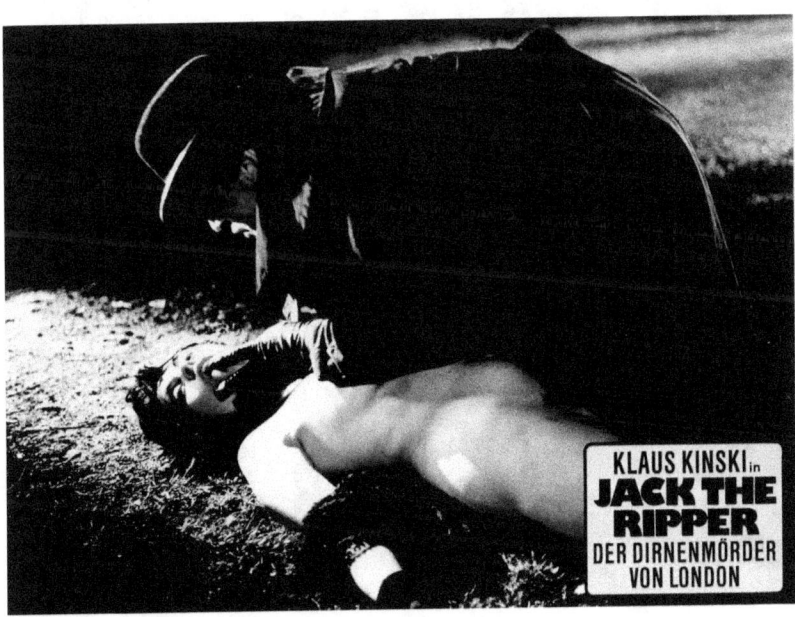

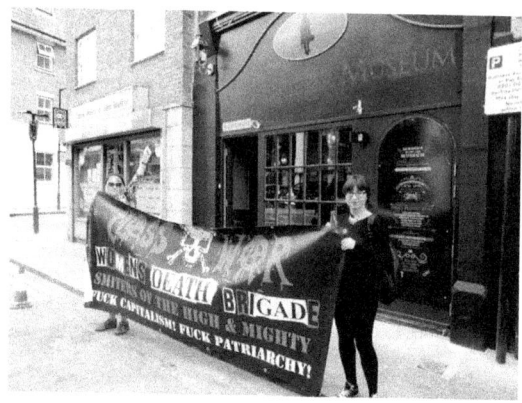

apparently the only real reason it's exposed to middle-class tantrums, but when it comes down to it, Jack the Ripper and London go way back. One more museum may be one too many for the posse, but it certainly won't be the last. (To name but one other, the London Dungeon has exhibited on the Ripper murders for decades, of course, but as a venue it's inconveniently large, successful and well-protected).

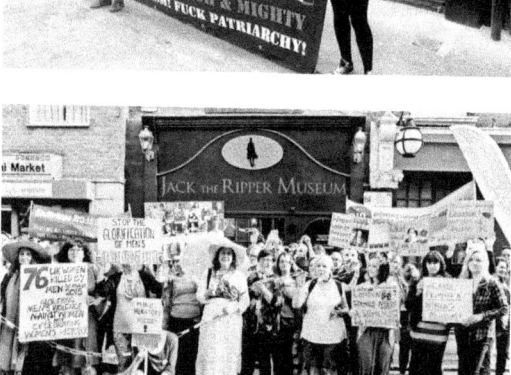

Fact is, 'gentrification' or not, the history of the East End is irrevocably caught up with vice, horror, death, disease, crime and unrest, and like it or not, the new JTRM is a part of the picture because that ever-uncaught murderer known as Jack the Ripper, and the women whose lives he cut short, are forever part of the East End too. London has long traded off its darkest heritage. You don't get to pick and choose which elements of this you like and which you don't based on some ill-founded whim. You don't get to police the world at weekends.

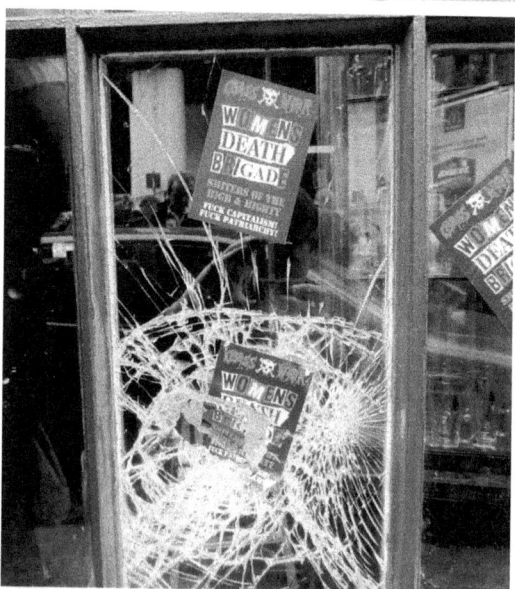

But here's the most important point about all of this, to my mind; to look at and to consider this dark heritage, and those swallowed up by it, is not necessarily to gawk and to misunderstand. To look at exhibits based on the women murdered by Jack the Ripper – is this to simply reduce them to nothing? For me, it was the opposite: several years ago, I visited a different JTR exhibition in London; it was an exhaustive array of artefacts associated with the case, arranged with care, and clearly the work of people who had thought

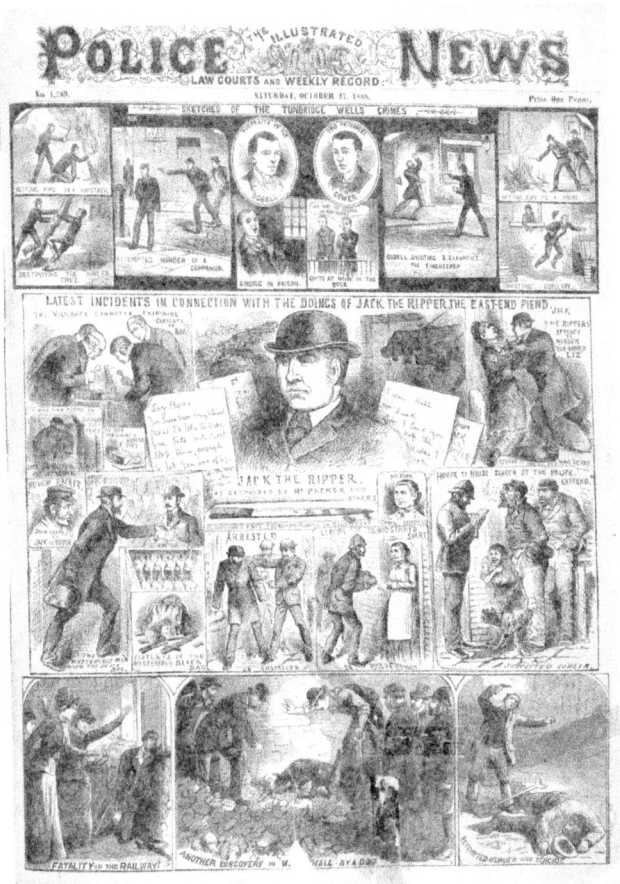

long and hard about what they wanted to achieve via their display. The result was something I found very moving indeed, and – sorry to contravene the narrative of the protest – deeply humanising. These were women, women who deserve so much more than simply to be a roll call of the deceased. Via the exhibition, they were given their identities back. This is what museums can achieve.

So why, then, are we told it is the case that to partake in the wrong kind of women's history is to reduce women like these to nothing? Maybe, just maybe, if you look at the JTRM logo and are so arrogant to think you know everything about the place itself, or so confident that an exhibition there reduces women to a red smudge and nothing more, or indeed if you look at a whistle and think of a rapist, then perhaps it is you who brings these oddball, uneasy sentiments to the table. Maybe you're the problem, and maybe you should turn that scrutinising eye – and megaphone – onto a worthwhile target.

end of part one
tv advertising and the way we were

Words: Ade Furniss

Mention the subject of television advertising to most people and their eyes are guaranteed to glaze over. In an age where much of what we watch is stored on a hard-drive, the commercial break is merely a minor nuisance, a cue to lift a lazy finger, hit fast forward on the digibox, and skip several adverts in one fell swoop. The fact is, since the advent of the VCR in the late 1970s, advertisers are fortunate if their sixty-second epics register with viewers on even a subliminal level. Perhaps surprisingly, despite the popularity of time-shift viewing, commercials remain big business, still funding the majority of television production in the Western world.

It's a stretch of the memory to recall a time when UK viewing options were limited to three channels, and the commercial break was an unavoidable passage between the 'parts' of every ITV programme; an era when TV advertising arguably had much greater influence and certainly a more prominent position in the national psyche. Many people in their middle-years will admit to a certain nostalgia for the more familiar adverts of yore: Leonard Rossiter spilling his Cinzano over Joan Collins; the intrepid lover with Milk Tray tucked under his arm; the PG Tips chimps' slapstick antics. Far more interesting, however, are the innumerable commercials that remain largely forgotten and yet submerged in the subconscious for years. Most have probably been lost to the ravages of times or buried in some corporate vault never to see the light of day again. However, thanks to early adopters of VCR technology and the wonders of YouTube, we can now travel back in time and indulge in that strange, warm sensation that comes with the sudden recollection of products, images, and music, memories of which had laid dormant in our minds for years.

For a nostalgic TV buzz, my personal preference is for the late 1970s/early 1980s and, as the commercials of that period prove, it was an era characterised by innovation and seismic scientific developments. Oven chips, for example. To witness the 1978 ad in which a 'comedy' French chef (portrayed by a familiar but unnameable Seventies character actor) presents a perfectly golden batch to the camera, with not a deep-fat fryer in sight, was to see history in

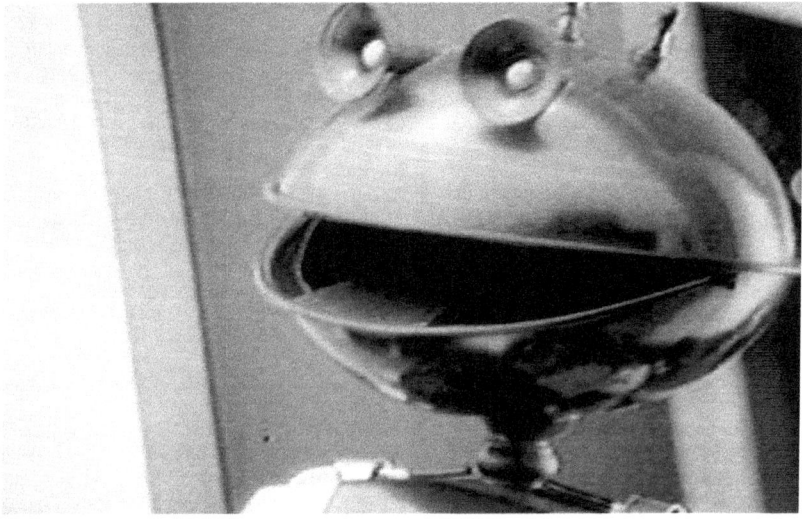

the making. No matter that the average home-cooked portion of oven chips is, to this day, an unappealing combination of carcinogenic cinder and raw potato. We were also ushered into Philips' *"video age"* as represented by a brown wooden box that would allow you access to Ceefax and its eyeball-grating text and graphics. And don't forget those remarkable Ronco products - yes, still being marketed as late as 1979! Always the dullard of the TV advertising world, the Ronco commercial was invariably an insultingly crude, shot-on-video effort. But who could resist the charms of their Flower Loom craft set and the ingenious record vacuum (*"It even takes 78s"*) when so ably demonstrated by an anonymous pair of hands and hawked by a booming Patrick Allen wannabe?

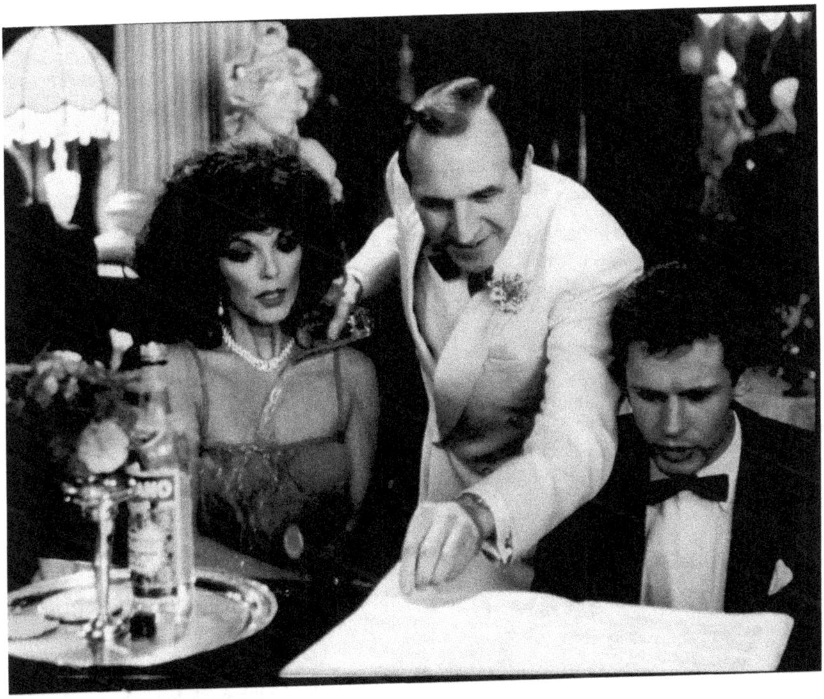

On a more sombre note, let us take a few moments to mourn some of those beloved snack products that are no longer with us. KP's Good & Crunchy crisps – promoted by cartoon wildlife and an insanely catchy jingle – came in packs that proudly boasted *"WITH BRAN"*. They were undoubtedly a huge hit with the chronically-constipated, but the rest of us found that they had an unpleasant

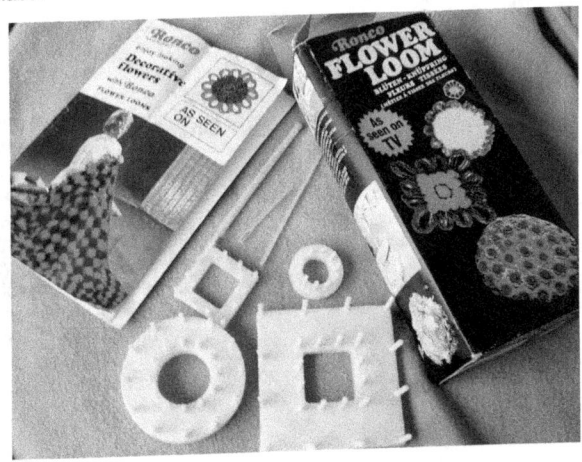

cardboardy texture, and the salt and vinegar variety was sufficiently acrid to inflict tongue lesions. Meanwhile, Banjos - as its mundane advert reminds us - were merely Blue Riband wafers with several peanut crumbs planted on top. Against competition from sexy newcomers like Gold bar (Caramac-covered biscuit) and United (with honeycomb, for Christ's sake!) such an underachiever never stood a chance. What about some Hanky Panky with Arthur Lowe? *"Necrophilia!"* you scream in disgust, and, funnily enough, poor Arthur is met with equal repulsion as he tries to tempt a dowdy spinster with his popcorn-based confectionary on a park bench. **Carry On** style humour abounds...as it does on a number of ads of the same vintage. Such a trip down memory lane isn't all fun though. The sight of gelatinous Chum dog food being slowly sliced in half is as nauseating as ever, and the accompanying interviews with pet owners remain tiresome even if the late 70s attire / hairdos do provide brief amusement. Based on my YouTube research, there also seemed to be an insatiable market for over-the-counter cough remedies during that time. Perhaps there's an interesting medical story about the nation's health to be told here, but the commercials are generally unimaginative, straight-faced, and reveal little about everyday life.

On the whole, there's something very soothing about watching adverts from this era. The reassuring narration – delivered by middle-aged, middle-class gents; some familiar (Richard Briers, Frank Windsor, Patrick Allen) others, regrettably, anonymous. The music was frothy and lightweight, with no concessions to contemporary pop music trends. An early ad for Discos crisps fails spectacularly to capitalise on the zeitgeist-seizing brand name, being soundtracked by something resembling a 1974 Wombles B-side. Perhaps the gentle paternal tone was a deliberate ploy to intoxicate a troubled nation with calming messages designed to create an association between product and peaceful contentment. Or maybe it was simply because the advertising world was governed by a generation who preferred things sedate and quaint. To hell with the punk revolution and militant strikers swarming outside the door!

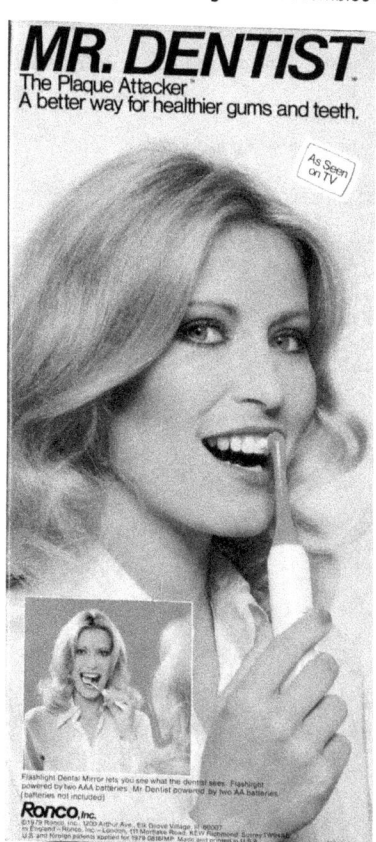

This isn't the place for an in-depth academic examination of advertising and its relationship with culture. Of course, it's a subject that has been thoroughly probed and picked apart by sociologists over many years. Suffice to say, watching anything created thirty years ago will highlight a wide variety of social changes, and I'd argue that, in this sense, adverts are more revealing than most other forms of media. Many adverts of the 78-81 era (and beyond) seek to engage us by depicting a credible domestic scenario to which the consumer can relate. Naturally, for mass appeal, it's essential that this reflects the core values of the age (although it can be argued that adverts also help shape and reinforce those values). Revealingly, the late Seventies ads are a politically-incorrect nightmare. Men are invariably depicted as adventurous and brave in their leisure pursuits and either sleekly professional or stoically industrious in their working lives. Women, on the other hand, do the ironing and serve Ross lasagne. While not quite as outrageously sexist as the ads from the previous decade, it's eye-opening stuff.

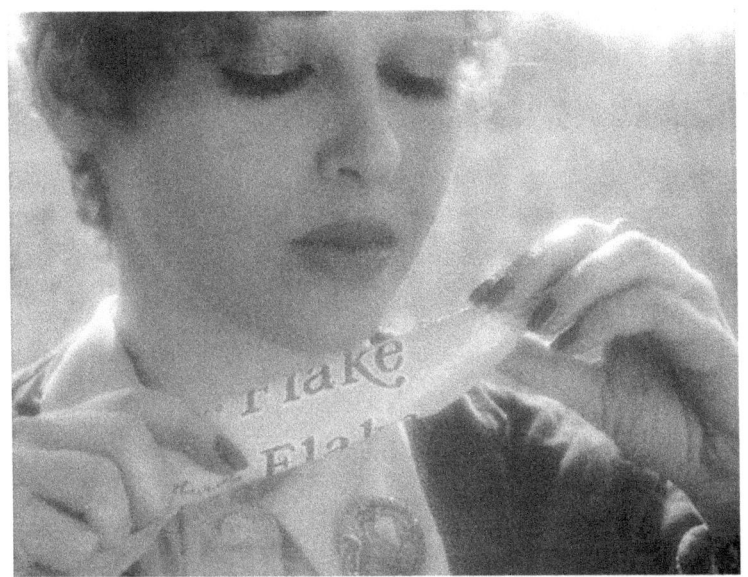

On a much more innocuous level, a multitude of minor changes to lifestyle norms are also exposed. A Heinz beans advert shows two young rascals playing conkers, one of them dodging a slight scuff to the forehead as his opponent takes a turn. Of course, yesterday's innocent fun has become an outlawed extreme sport in the playgrounds of 2016. These days we drink Lucozade so that we can stay hydrated during marathons but back in the late Seventies it was seen as a quasi-medicinal product that *"aids recovery"*. It was expensive, drunk sparingly and only when you were ill, and the bottle came wrapped in orange plastic film for some unknown reason. As a rich source of nostalgia and education , it's a crime that we don't seem to appreciate historical TV advertising as we should. The preservation of TV commercials and the ability for us to access them is too important to be left in the hands of a few YouTube uploaders*

Sadly, as I understand, any attempt to release DVD compilations of vintage commercials would prove to be a copyright minefield. Unfortunately, despite the special place that old commercials have in many hearts, sales are unlikely to justify the considerable outlay.

* No disrespect intended. Their efforts are definitely appreciated.

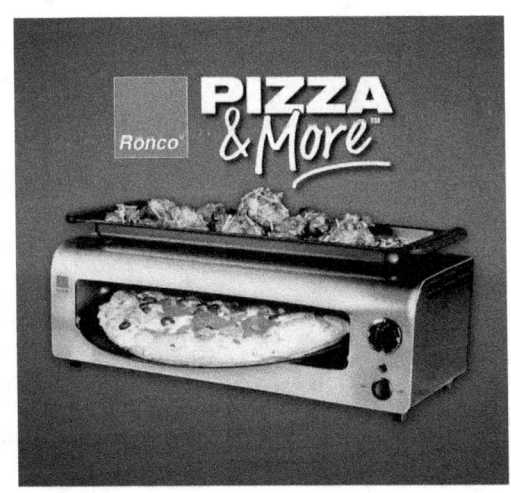

i'm not defending rape porn, but...

Words: Hayden Hewitt

...I kind of am going to defend it, which is rather odd given that I honestly don't get it. Saying that there are many fetishes and fantasies I don't really get or understand how you could derive pleasure from them. Thing is, it's none of my business what consenting adults get up to in the privacy of their own heads, bedrooms, or torture dungeons come to that and it's none of yours either. Most of all it shouldn't be any of the government's affair.

A few years ago, the ban on 'extreme pornography' was extended by our enlightened leaders to include the genre of rape porn. Let's clarify something off the bat: rape porn is carried out by consenting adults role-playing the scenario of forced sexual congress. Seems pretty awful to most but there are quite a lot of people, both men and women, who fantasise about such things. This doesn't mean they want to actually rape or be raped, they just get a sexual kick out of the general idea. At no point does rape porn involve actual rape. Are such fantasies 'sick'? I suppose it depends on your point of view really and your point of view should never extend to telling other people how to think or what should tickle their sexual pickle. Here is the actual legislation:

In a new Report, the Joint Committee on Human Rights welcomes the provision in the Criminal Courts and Justice Bill, carried over from the last Session of this Parliament, which extends the current offence of possession of extreme pornography to include possession of

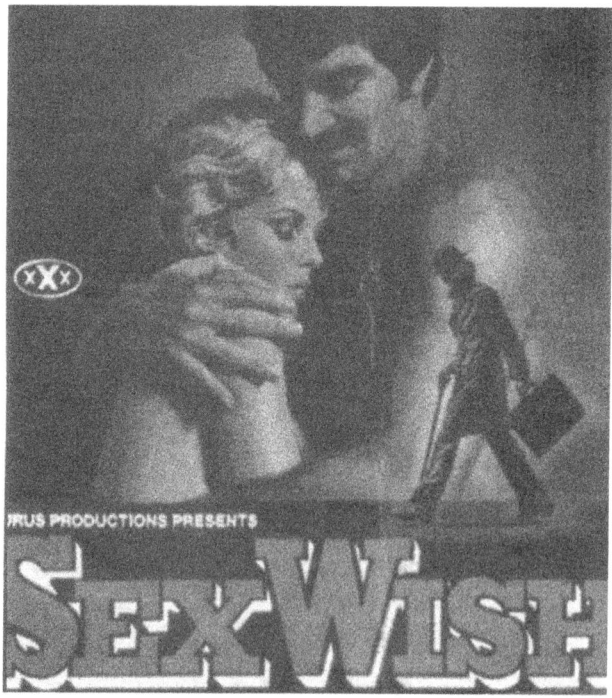

pornographic images depicting rape and other non-consensual sexual penetration. The Committee considers this provision to be human rights enhancing, given the evidence of cultural harm done by such pornography, and acknowledges the strong justification provided by the Government and others for this proportionate restriction on individual rights.

Does that make sense to you? What catches the eye is the part of the article reading *"The Committee considers this provision to be human rights enhancing"*. I'm very interested to know exactly whose human rights are enhanced by this legislation. How are any human rights enhanced by the banning of fictional acts of role-playing carried out by consenting adults? I can understand that it would please anti-porn campaigners or perhaps people who consider anything they find disgusting as suitable fodder to be banned, but enhancing human rights? No, I can't see that at all.

Then we have the killer line *"given the evidence of cultural harm done by such pornography"*. Now this is a good part; firstly I'd like to know what evidence there is. What research has been done on rape porn and its effects on our culture? Where is the general consensus on this? Furthermore, what culture exactly? Not only is this sentence untrue in terms of 'evidence' it's also a nonsense invoking 'culture' in such a manner as to render the word meaningless. Come to think on it 'cultural harm' is an entirely meaningless phrase anyway; it still gets the heads nodding from the ban camp though I would imagine.

Not only that - but is our culture so very fragile, so easily distorted, that a small subgenre of pornography could cause it harm? I don't have any hard statistics on this but I'll go out on a limb here and point out that this form of porn probably doesn't show up in search engine results all that often compared to most although I wouldn't take a bet against such fantasies being a little more popular than most of us would be comfortable with, regardless of how harmless such fantasies are.

This smacks of yet more appeasement. The extreme pornography law was brought in following the actions of one despicable human being who was found to enjoy such things and the media had a field day. There's no evidence rape porn does any cultural harm whatsoever, there's no evidence that the people who watch it will turn to rape (statistically I'd say the evidence shows exactly the opposite by a huge margin), in fact nobody really cared about rape porn at all until some moral crusaders decided Aunty Government should ban it so that all of us weak-willed buffoons don't suddenly turn into a nation of rapey monsters. It's good to know that in the face of the lack of any kind of decent research, any proof it's harmful, the government still feel it's acceptable to remove it and feel justified to put in place this 'proportionate restriction on individual rights' because it's for our own good.

Still, it doesn't matter though does it? I mean, who on earth is going to defend rape porn?

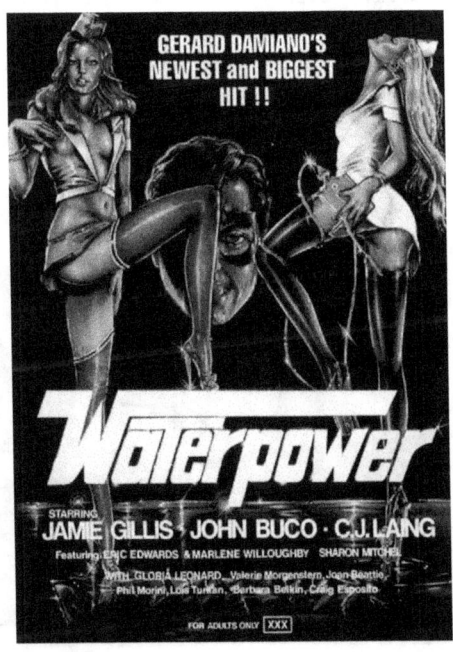

from the sacred to the profane
sex, scent and sensuality

Words: Gipsie Castiglione

You probably have a couple of bottles of perfume lying around, or maybe you are a bit of an addict. But how much do you actually know about the stuff sitting in your bathroom or bedroom? It still shocks me how little thought most people give to choosing the perfumes they wear. Considering not only the amount of information they tell our peers about us, but also how hypnotic and bewitching their power can be to potential paramour, you would think that such choices would be as carefully considered as our clothing picks. But no, the majority of us seem content to pick up something cheap at the airport on the way to loungey days full of the promise of slow skin cancer procurement on tropical beaches, and hedonistic nights in boozy garish night clubs. Even worse is the dreaded Christmas or birthday gift – it's one thing to choose a bargain on impulse, but having no choice at all is ghastly! I couldn't think of a crueler torture than having to wear some insipid monstrosity that is someone else's fantasy of my alter ego, another person's idea of my personality. It should be forbidden - unless of course it is within the bounds of a Dom-Sub affair, when the forced use of a specific scented potion could be most satisfactory or unsettling depending on the role.

Perfume has secreted its way into our psyche since time immemorial; many of the precious raw materials having been here long before us, like roses, which have habituated earth for over 35 million years. The Egyptians were the first civilization to unleash the power of scented elements, resins, shrubs and woods... burnt as an appreciation of their deities, a fragrant 'thank you' ignited on humble earth, from which the smoke emitted rose to the heavens, the residency of all things celestial and godly. This is where the word perfume originally comes from - *per fumum* in Latin, meaning 'through smoke'.

This instantly pleasing aroma in the temples would have also permeated the clothes, hair and skin of the worshippers, and there you have the eureka moment: not only would the environment have seemed more pleasant and magical, but the sensations from the purifying element would have made them feel spiritually closer to their deities too.

Go forward in history a little. Why do Christian churches - in fact most places of worship whatever creed they may be - burn incense? Yes, there is still the symbolic gratitude, but perhaps the alleviation of the stench of all the gathered pilgrims (who after their long journeys in search of holy absolution, must have been more than a little noxious smelling) was a factor too. Either way, these gifts - worthy of a new born King - bring us a little closer to Elysium, to our higher selves...

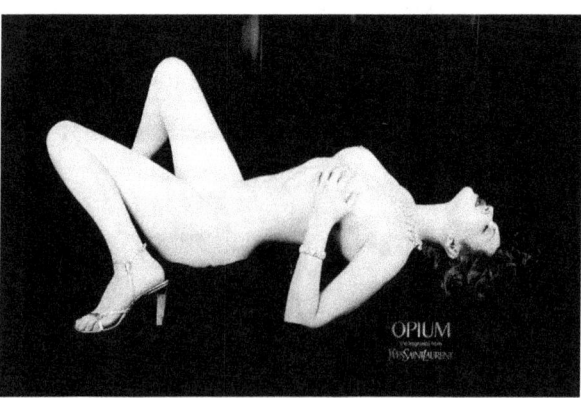

In Islamic cultures the tradition of using smoke to perfume the home's environment and oneself is still popular, a gesture called bakhoor. I once heard a story that some of the higher rankling royals have Agar wood (which Oud oil is extracted from) bakhoors that cost around £4000 a time.

It didn't take long for someone to work out that these powerfully evocative scents could be used to influence more than just the gods. This is also the main reason we wear perfume - seduction. Let's face it, we spend a hell of a lot of time working out ways to get laid, and perfume has been a part of seduction and erotic rites for millennia. Think of Cleopatra, who is said to have scented the veils of her boat so that her chosen prey would be captivated before her arrival - now that lady new how to make an entrance. Can you imagine what wildly X-rated potions would have been mixed for our first beauty guru?

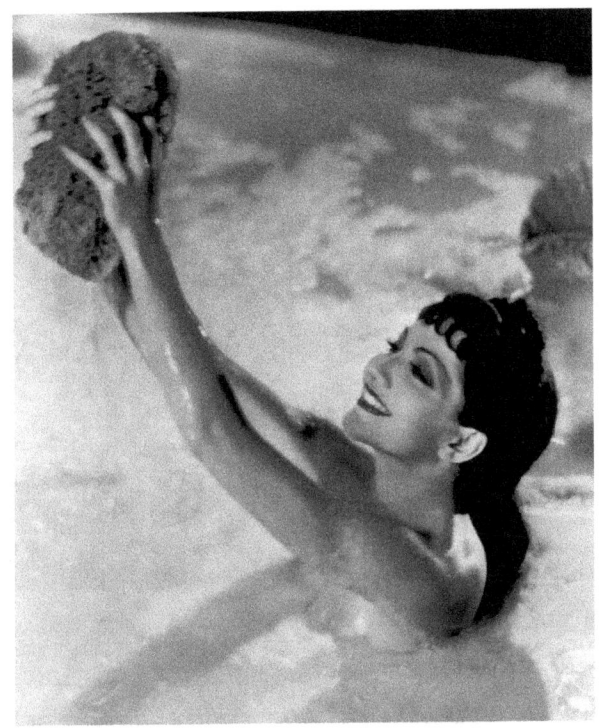

The Phoenicians, Greeks and Romans took it to new levels. The Greeks were the first to crush aromatic material to infuse oils with, the sole purpose of which was to scent their skin, and rival the dwellers of Olympus. In India and the middle east, the tradition of Attars - perfumed oils - is still strong, and very much Influencing western perfumery. Alas, we are so strictly governed here, the legality of these in Europe is very dubious – a pity as the good ones can be quite magnificent (you can find very cheap ones in markets everywhere, but they are best left there). The Phoenicians traded it to the Romans, who - ever the decadents - even scented the wings of birds, and then released them during their festivities to accelerate the Bacchanalian mood of the soirée.

Throughout history we have heroes and heroines who championed perfume, and added their own chapters to the story. Catherine de Medici, the infamous French Catholic queen and ever the femme fatale, knew better than to ever leave her native Florence without her perfumer Rene de Florentine, who also was her poison conjurer. She made perfumed gloves, Florentine Iris and even eau de cologne fashionable in France and the rest of Europe, and immortalised the idea of the evil, beautiful vamp with secret, poison-filled jewels. We can only dwell on the thought of the scents of other iconic femme fatales like Eve, and Salome, but I bet the snake in the garden of Eden offered more than a mere apple to tempt mankind into damnation....

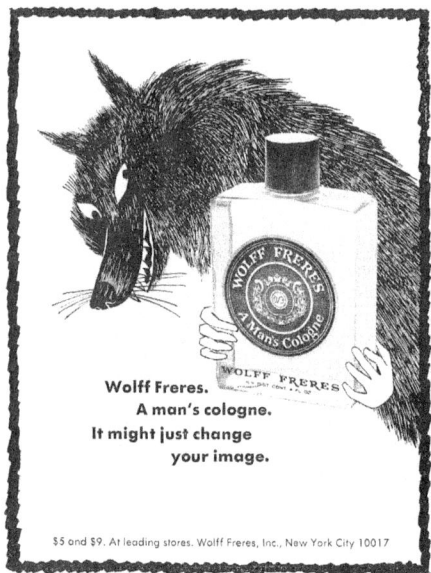 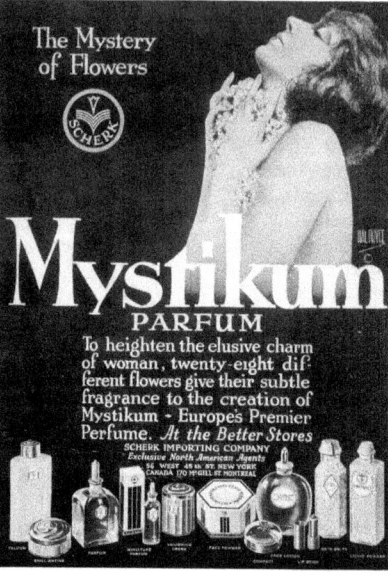

The notoriety of perfume as a poison and a sign of wickedness still continues today - in some cultures, a perfume that is too strong or too recognisable can immediately give the wearer a reputation as a person of infamy!

The names perfumes are given are a massive hint to the power that lies within the amber liquids. In the Golden age of perfumery - the art deco years - we had jewels like *Narcise Noir, Tabac Blonde, Bandit, Tabu, Fetish* and *Scandal*, while decades later we were offered *Opium, Poison, Obsession* - you get the picture. The 1970s and 1980s were perhaps the most outrageous, Revlon gave us *Charlie*, the Cosmo girl who was so emancipated that she was tirelessly running around town pinching men's bottoms. Men's advertising campaigns really kicked ass in those days - adonises coming out of the surf in so many ads, it's hard to recall them all, (though strangely the perfumes rarely smell of this salty water promise they elude). The most memorable ad campaigns have to be *Denim*, with that feminine hand sliding through chest hair on a downward journey of carnal discovery, and Valerie Leon as the maneater in *Hai Karate*. These two promised the wearer not only irresistibility alone, but that sex was guaranteed. How we miss those days of political incorrectness - we are all far too easily offended these days, and there is no humour and precious little animal sex left at all, despite the controversy-baiting efforts of the likes of Tom Ford.

Except here at **The Reprobate**, of course. We remain intrigued by the weaknesses of the flesh, decadent behaviour and not denying ourselves any pleasures that may come our way, be they mad, bad or dangerous. We'll leave the supposed virtues of subtle, feel good colognes to lesser magazines. Our perfume desires are mostly made of the darker, the exotic, the more unyielding material - although every so often we know how to use the power of a subtle molecule that wears close to the skin, draws you in, and talks to the subconscious.

How to master the art of scent seduction you ask? Well, ask you may… it is a long passionate journey, one filled with as many mysteries as lie amongst the strange and curious ingredients within the elixirs themselves. It is very much like the consumable kind of alcohol – making a choice is a lot more complex than simply going for the most appealing bottle, even if we have all occasionally fallen foul of that misdemeanour. Such mistakes can be very costly, in more ways than one.

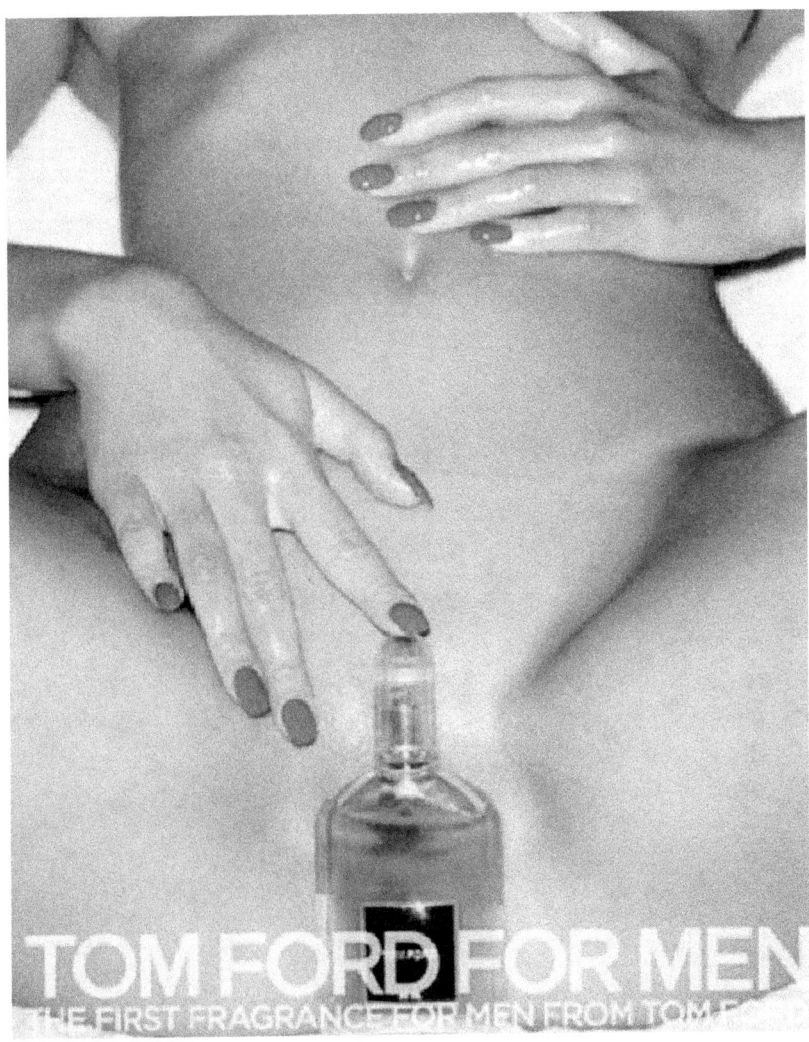

Before being concerned with what turns others on, start by finding out what makes you fall head over heels with your own skin. I would normally guide you straight over to the Orientals, Spices and Animalics for the purpose of seduction, but these are acquired tastes. It takes me back to an event a few years ago, when a very well-known cougar from a certain fashion and sex obsessed TV show based in New York, said *"darling, help me find the sexiest perfume in the World"*. Immediately, we went to Editions de Parfum, and sampled *Musc Ravageur* – the name says it all, dear reader. It was received like a slap across the face, as it turned out the blonde Venus was really looking for a very lady-like perfume, full of roses and incense - very beautiful, but not the sex crazed, power defying signature she thought she ought to be portraying. It was a fascinating moment to observe.

Being irresistible, sexy and alluring is all about confidence, so whatever you choose remember this: you must wear it, not it wear you. That expression of being comfortable in your own skin was coined for a reason! You can't fake it with perfume. So discover what you love, what makes you feel as though you can conquer anyone with your charm and devilish ways. Once you have your groove, then start to get weird until one day you can totally rock a kinky, dark, smoky oud, or blacker than black leather, or indeed the diva of all divas, the tuberose.

It's worth noting is that your perfume is like an invisible halo - it talks on your behalf, and it alludes to your alter ego, your true self, or the role you wish to play at that moment. It greets people around you silently but surely, leaving behind an impression of you sometimes long after you have gone. First and last impressions are worth taking time over - you can never repeat them after all - and most certainly can seal or sour the deal.

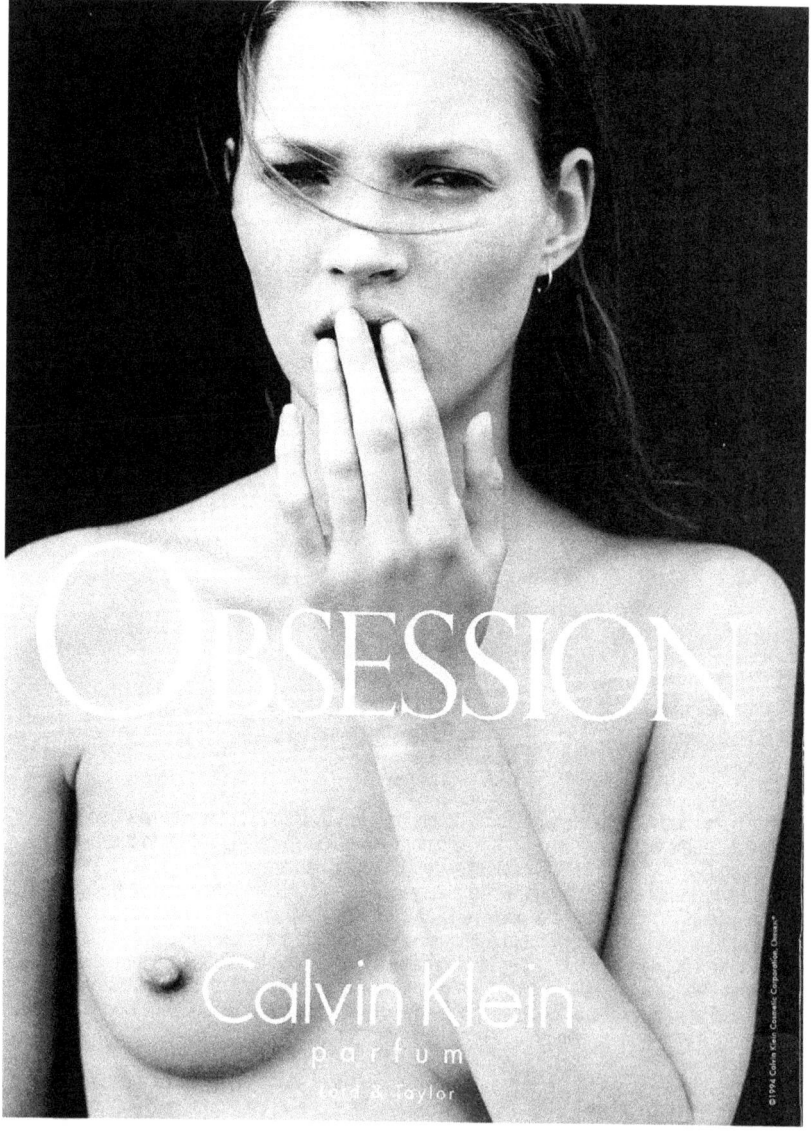

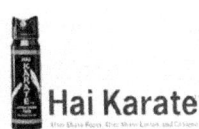

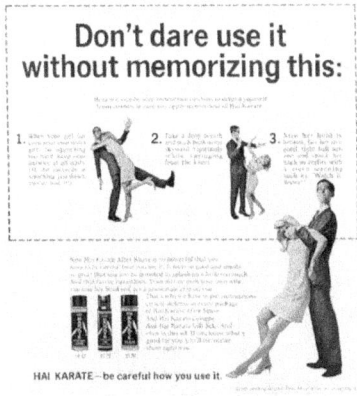

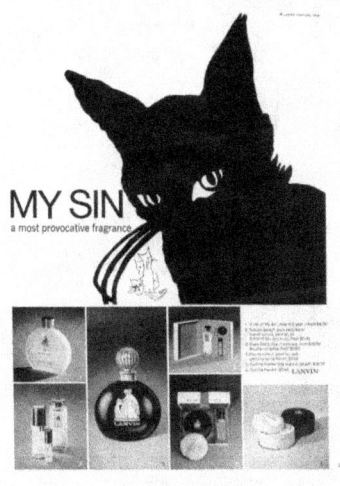

Here is a very quick guide to some of the families, and ingredient types, and a few of my favourite examples in the categories. May I please note at this point, that there is not a definite bible of perfumery - whoever you listen to, no one will tell you the same thing. Perfume is filled with ambiguity, so take it all in, play around and make your own mind up:

Hespederics (or Citruses) are full of joy, sparkle and get up and go, and like most good things are very fleeting. *Oranges & Lemons Say the Bells of St Clements* by Heeley, *Eau de Fleurs de Cedrat* by Guerlain, *Bergamot Soleil* by Atelier Cologne, and *Eau de Lisbon* by Angela Flanders.

Orientals are exotic, seductive and dreamy, tend to linger and announce you and can be very addictive. My favourite amber accords can be found in this family (not to be confused with amber gris) - *Flame of Gold* by Orlov, *Opium* by Yves Saint Laurent, *Shalimar* by Guerlain (for the last two I am referring to the originals, not the washed out versions we have to put up with today), *Amber Noir* by Angela Flanders, the utterly bewitching *Dark Heart of Old Havana* by 4160 Tuesdays, *Salome* by Papillon (a real favourite of the moment with the perfumistas), and *Alamut* by Lorenzo Villoresi.

Normally classified under oriental, but I feel they deserve their own category: *Resins* or the tears of the desert (Myrrh, Frankincense, Labdanum...) are supernatural, influential, confident. *Phoenicia* and *Cardinal* both by Heeley, *Larmes Du Désert* by Atelier des Ors, *La Liturgie des Heures* by Jovoy.
Woods have strength, are confident and reassuring, and there is a huge variety to explore. *French Lover* by Editions de Parfums, *Dry Wood* by Ramon Monegal, *Sandalo* by Lorenzo Villoresy, *Femininito de Bois* by Serge Lutens are all fine examples.

Mossy or green notes (like oakmoss) are natural yet provocative and intrepid. Try *Precious One* by Angela Flanders, *Bandit* by Robert Piguet, *Chypre 21* by Heeley.

Florals are as varied as they are alluring. They can convey tenderness, ardent passion, eroticism, extravagance, elegance, grace, infinite variety, and are not just for the girls - a dab of tuberose on a man an be irresistible. In fact perfume is really genderless, despite the hard efforts of the big companies. To tell you otherwise. Don't believe the hype, wear whatever you like! *Une Rose* by Editions de Parfum, *Fracas* by Robert Piguet - inspired by Rita Hayworth in **Gilda** - *Iris de Nuit* by Heeley (the auteur says Irises smell of angels, also the most expensive oil in perfumery) *Gardez Moi* by Jovoy, *Narcise Noir* by Caron, *Gold* by Amouage, *Gardenia* by Isabey, *Chanel 22* - personally I find it more wearable than 5 and it is also full of aldehydes,

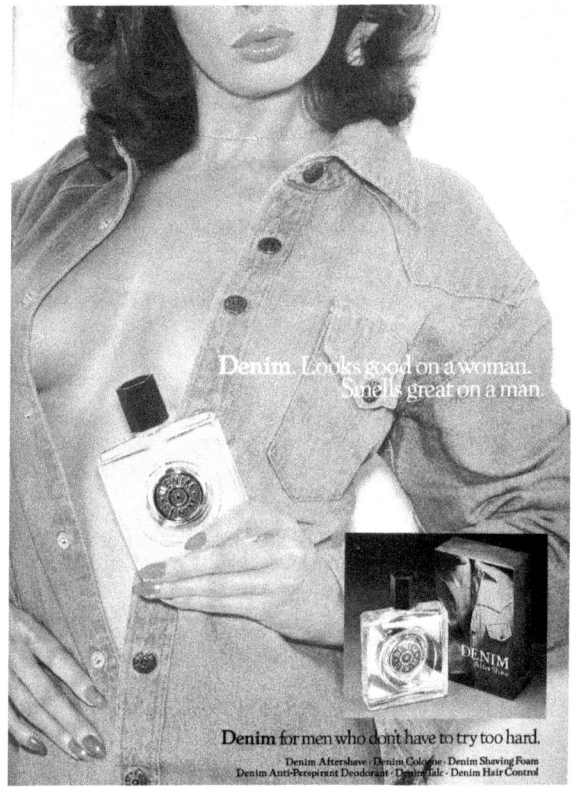

which are the secret to both, a wonderful early synthetic that makes flowers sing. I find it almost more interesting than the ingredients it's supposed to enhance. Try John Galliano's *Signature* which has an overdose of it - I'm not sure it's still available, but well worth tracking down, and probably very cheap. Agent Provocateur's *Maitresse* was also a very gorgeous and sexy aldehyde experiment·

Spices are spicy, sexy, downright outrageous sometimes, and most likely to carry a XXX rating, especially cinnamon and nutmeg (of course not on every skin, but that is the discovery journey). *Musc Ravageur* by Editions de Parfum, *L`Air du Desert Marocain* by Andy Tauer, *Aziyade* by Parfum d'Empire, *Lyric Men* by Amouage.

Animal ingredients are in almost every bottle you will pick up, as they are the key fixatives (fix all other ingredients to your skin). Most are now synthetic, with Musk and Amber Gris the most popular, civet and castoreum the wildest and less used. They can range from smelling like natural, clean, powdery skin, to dirty and fecal. *Tient de Niege* by Lorenzo Villoresi, *Rouge 540* by Francis Kurkdjian, *Muscs Koublai Khan* by Serge Lutens (Paris only), *Absolue pour le soir* by Francis Kurkdjian - this last one is a magnificent beast that sadly is being phased out, and being literally censored. Look for the older bottles that smell really animalistic (the new version is not available yet) it has a generous dose of civet (although not often mentioned) for that extra hardcore night of wild abandonment the perfumer was trying to evoke.

Leathers, Tobaccos and Ouds manifest fetishistic, dominant traits. *Knize 10* by Knize, *Oud* by Maison Francis Kukdjian, *Tabac Blonde* by Caron, *Lonestar Memories* by Andy Tauer and *Black Afgano* by Nasomatto are all fabulously decadent. A word on Oud - it has been the ingredient de jour for over a decade now, so popular that south east Asia (where the much sought after substance comes from) has run out of the wild variety - only the farmed type is left, and it's still prohibitively expensive. It is a category on its own right now, and there are more varieties available that there should be. It can get very geeky, and a lifetime quest for some!

Marines & Oceanics smell like the air and the sea. I would say don't bother, but some new ones can give quite a nice salty skin finish, if surf babe is one of your guises. *Sel Marine* by Heeley is the only one I can really, honestly recommend.

Gourmands smell like candy and are full of childhood memories - a little can be great, too much is only for eight year olds. *Musc Maori* by Parfumerie Generale is a great example; 4160 Tuesdays use gourmand ingredients in very interesting and pleasing ways, and I imagine you're probably familiar with *Angel* by Thierry Mugler, the one that started it all.

Fruits (the non-citrus kind) convey fun, playfulness, are quite irresistible if used correctly. *Poison* by Dior (original), *Figue Noir* by Angela Flanders, *Philosykos* by Diptyque, and *Aventus* by Creed.

Fougeres (Ferns) are the most virile, mostly featuring lavender – yes, the stuff granny keeps in her draw!! Trust me: Lavender in perfume is all about the male! *Caron pour un homme* is the best example, in the top 100 bestselling men's scents since 1937, and worn by Cary Grant, Gerard Depardieu, Roger Moore, Tom Ford, Serge Gainsbourg and almost every French president. *Pluriel* by Francis Kukdjian is a fab modern take on it, as is *Aberdeen Lavender* by Creed and *Azzaro pour homme*.

Most perfumes are a mixture of several families, which means like the mixing of words, musical notes and paint pigments the possibilities are endless.

The best way to go about trying new scents is first on a blotter, and if you are still intrigued after a few minutes then commit some skin to it. Note that a perfume on a blotter is like a dress or a suit on a hanger. It needs skin to bring it to life, and time - at least 30 minutes, ideally four hours. Don't bother spraying the back of your hand, it's never very nice there. The best place to try is the wrist, and the inside of your elbow, and if you are very bendy you could try the back of the knees, as they are perfect. Leave the back of the neck, navel and décolletage for one of your victims to lust over. Oh, and don't rub your wrists together - that ruins the 3D experience cleverly constructed in the lab by the perfumer. Also, be as charming as you can be to the consultant in the shop, and you may be given some rare precious sample vials to try later, perhaps whilst on a date, or a new role playing scene with your regular squeeze. The sales consultants get a lot of stick from perfumistas - depending where you are, they will be a fount of knowledge or sadly have very little if any (no fault of their own, they are paid to dish out the

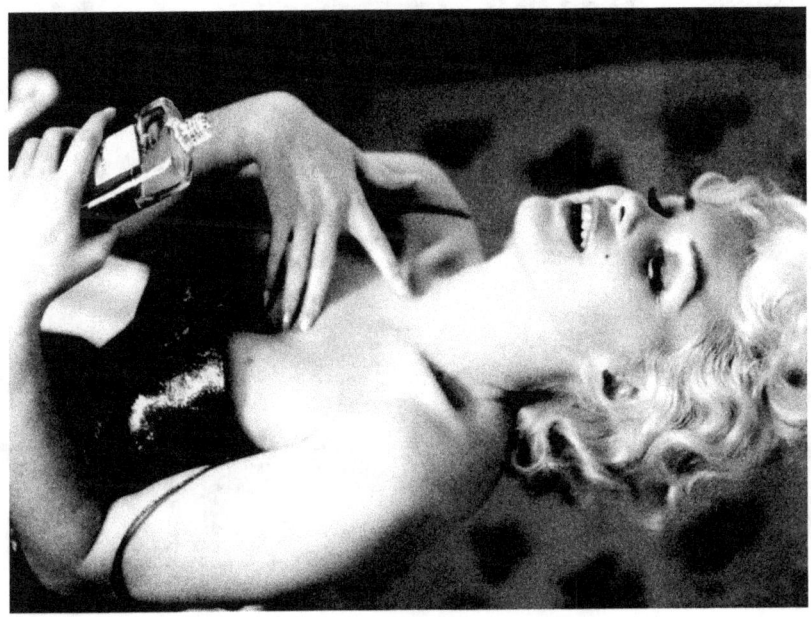

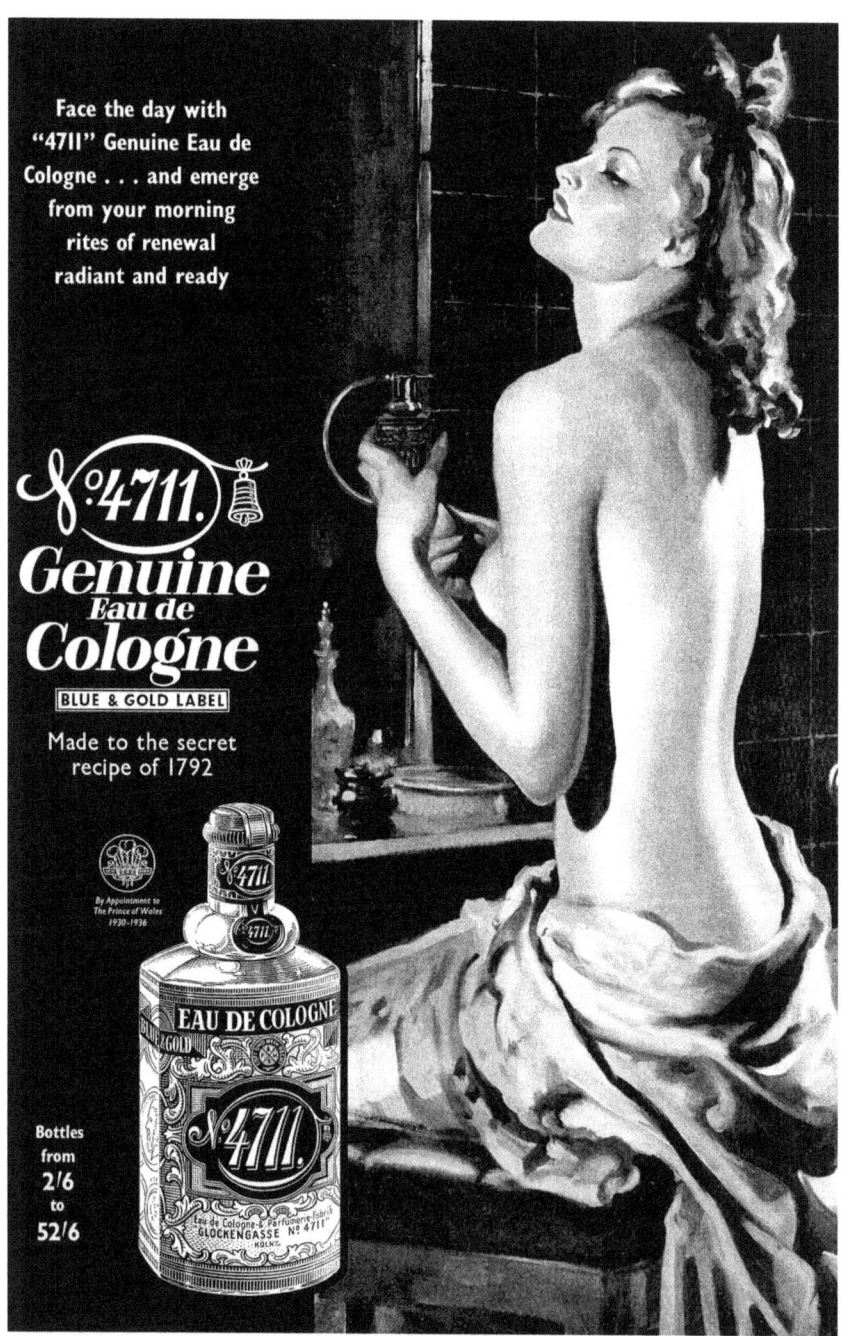

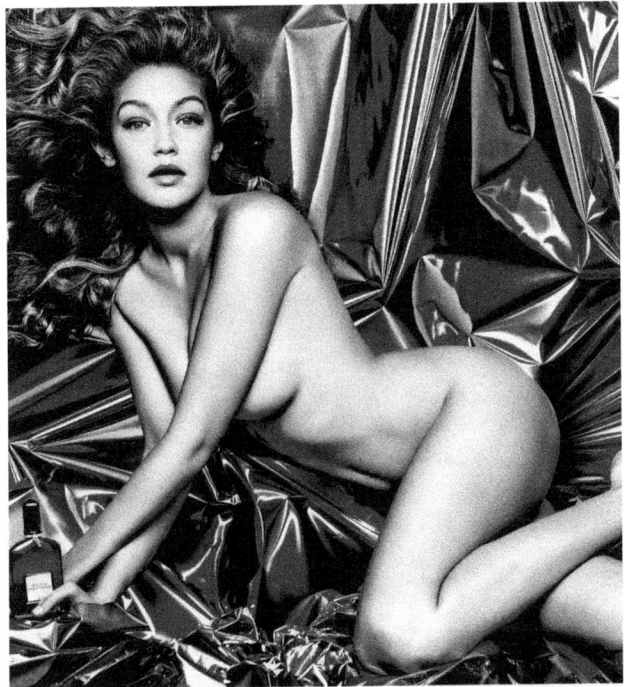

companies lines, and may have no interest in the subject. Most have huge sales targets to achieve so can sometimes be very pushy, but don't let them talk you into buying there and then - make 'perfume can't be rushed' a mantra.

I once read a review - never ever trust anyone's opinion but your own - about an innovative, total left field, explicit perfume called *Secretions Magnifique* - again the name says it all. How could the smell of blood, sweat, adrenaline and semen not be delicious? While on a business trip to Birmingham with a few colleagues, we happened upon it in Harvey Nichols. Excitement went to my head and I liberally sprayed the little kinky monster on. 10 minutes in, I was a psychotic mess - I smelt as if I'd been throwing myself a around an abattoir like a possessed Linda Blair. I'm not sure what death smells like, but I'm pretty sure this was close to it, and not a nice Victorian vampire style death either - this beast was foul, without an ounce of romance and a lot of plasma! My boss had to put me in a cab, thinking I was a loon, premenstrual or both, so I could go to my hotel and shower as much of the pong off as I could. Let that be a warning: know what you are putting on your skin or possibly live to regret it. Funnily enough, on some luckier souls *SM* - yes, the Initials are quite poignant! - smells like innocent sparkling violets are draped on the wearers skin, so I dare you - go and try it...

Be warned: short-lived scent affairs can be a very costly mistresses. The sales consultant will most probably tell you that their potions are full of only the most rarest and expensive ingredients mother nature has to offer, and we shall not get into the natural versus synthetic argument right now, but as Frederic Malle perfectly puts it, *"a very good perfume will be made up of both"*. The fact is that the powers that be are making it harder to use naturals in perfumery all the time. You may drink as much orange juice as you wish, but your friendly local perfumer – should they wish to sell in Europe - will be very limited as to how much citrus oil they can use in their formula. Synthetics are also wonderful, they give infinite creative freedom, and will most likely never give you an allergic reaction, but long live both!

Go, have fun, it's a wild ride if you do it properly!

death as art, art as death

Words: Nigel Wingrove

A few years ago when Damien Hirst was contemplating making his first ten million and Tracy Emin was still using her bed to sleep in, a young artist called Mark Quinn unveiled a sculpture of his face made from four and half litres of his own blood which had been frozen into a cast of his head. Titled *Self*, it was immediately bought by art collector Charles Saatchi for a reputed £13,000 (in April 2005 the work was sold to a US collector for £1.5 million) and brought horror as art into the mainstream media.

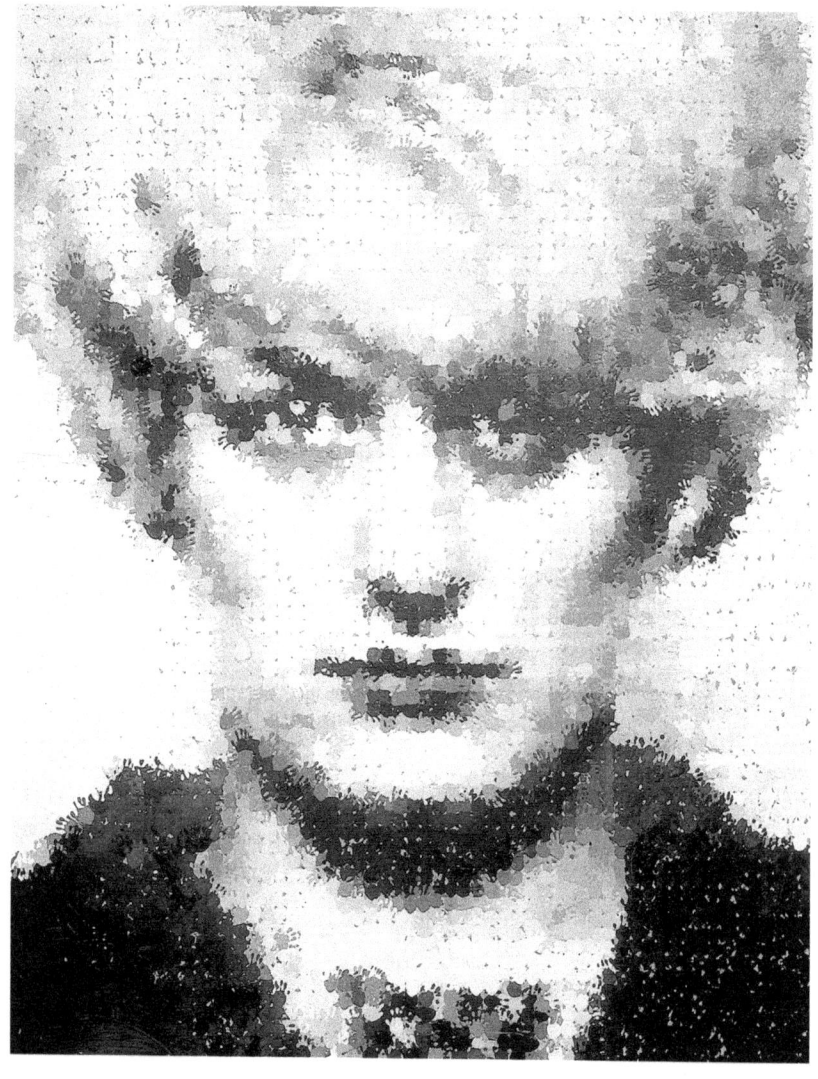

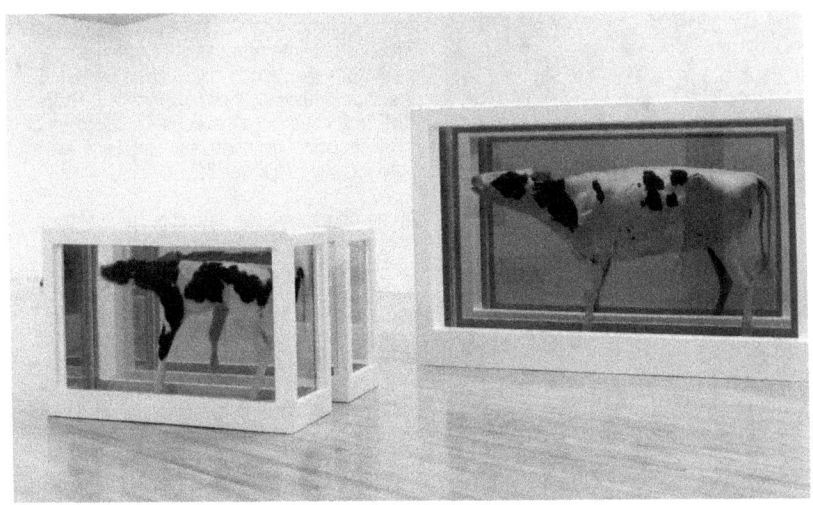

The art mainstream though, and Charles Saatchi in particular, were already well into horroresque with Saatchi having reputedly turned up at Damien Hirst's first warehouse show, *Modern Medicine and Gambler* (1991), and been gobsmacked by Hirst's first major animal installation, *A Thousand Years*, which consisted of a large glass case filled with live maggots and flies feeding off a rotting cow's head, a piece that was also bought by Saatchi. Hirst famously followed this up with a shark in formaldehyde called *The Physical Impossibility of Death in the Mind of Someone Living* (1992) and, most notoriously of all, *Mother and Child Divided* (1993), in which a cow and her calf were cut into sections and exhibited in a series of separate glass cabinets. Art became X-rated and as shocking as any Video Nasty.

Art was now expected to be in-your-face and artists often seemed to vie with one another in the gross-out stakes with work after work seeming to up the anti, whether in terms of offence, outrageousness or horror. British artist Marcus Harvey's work *Myra* (1995), in which children's hand prints using shades of black and grey recreated the iconic police photograph of child-killer Myra Hindley into a huge portrait caused outrage and consternation when it was premiered at the Royal Academy as part of the *Sensation Exhibition* and for many this was an exhibition too far.

Sensation was in fact an exhibition determined to live up to its name as, alongside *Myra*, were the enfants pornographic - life size mannequins of naked children, the creation of brothers Jake and Dinos Chapman. Their pre-pube figures were almost Manga-esque representations of childhood innocent and purity, except they had penis noses, or penises inserted into their anuses or vaginas or both and the effect was unnerving

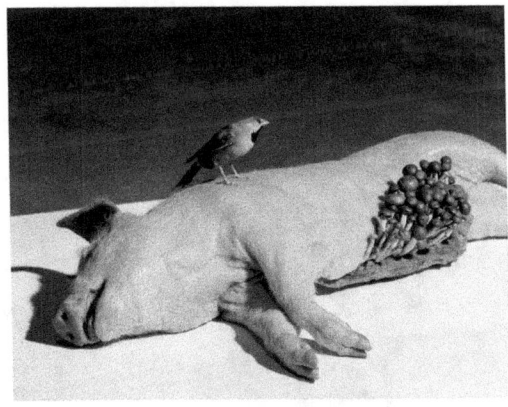

47

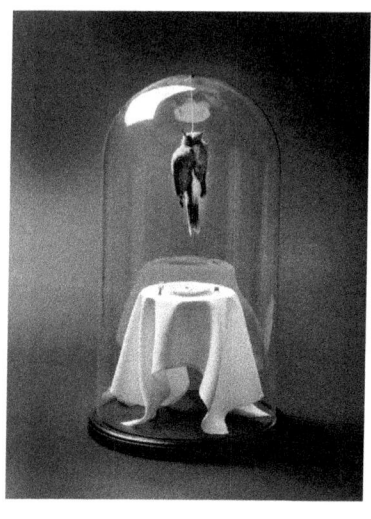

and unsettling. Again outrage followed outrage. Protests became scary as the mother of one of the Moor's Murderer's child victims protested the show and windows were smashed. The BBC described the exhibition as a collection of 'gory images of dismembered limbs and explicit pornography'. This was the Art Nasty.

Art as 'shock and awe' in fact became almost the norm with artists becoming like rock stars earning enormous sums of money and causing outrage as their works toured the world. But, like horror in film, what shocked once soon loses its power and equally, like rock and pop, what appealed one week soon bores the next and so it is with art. Soon, frozen heads, severed limbs and genital representations of religious figures seemed dated and tired. And death, like everything else in celebrity culture, art included, found that it had to reinvent itself if it wanted to stay on top.

Now over ten years on from *Sensation*, penis-faced children and Hirst's mutilated farm animals, we have seen death and the dead making a comeback in the form of taxidermy and a young female artist called Polly Morgan. Morgan's work has been attracting praise and delighting art critics with her dark, macabre and often humorous interpretations of death, contrasting with the often brutalised visions of the previous decades art Shock Troopers.

Morgan has reinvented taxidermy and, at the same time, taken it back to its roots in Victorian England where taxidermists often portrayed animals at play in Beatrice Potter style costumes or in macabre settings often with different species joined to create bizarre hybrids. The new wave of art taxidermists are not seeking as the Victorians often did to recreate life from the dead but rather to bring life to their dead. So in Morgan's work *Still Life After Death (rabbit)* (2006) for instance, a magician's black top hat floats high above a 'dead' white rabbit effectively reversing their traditional roles. Likewise in *Still Life After Death (fox)* (2006), a fox is shown sleeping in the bowl of an outsized champagne glass.

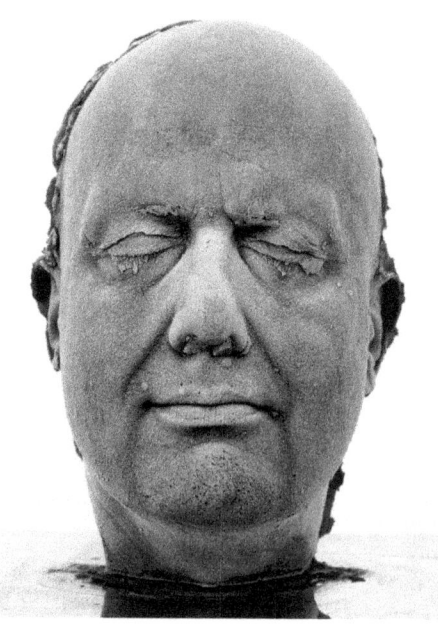

Or, in the piece *Morning* (2007), a robin is shown smashing through a window, mixing black humour with an acknowledgement that the animal is dead and not undead.

Yet Morgan's work is dark and getting darker. In *Former Things* (2007), a **Ring** like woman sits head and black hair hung forwards,

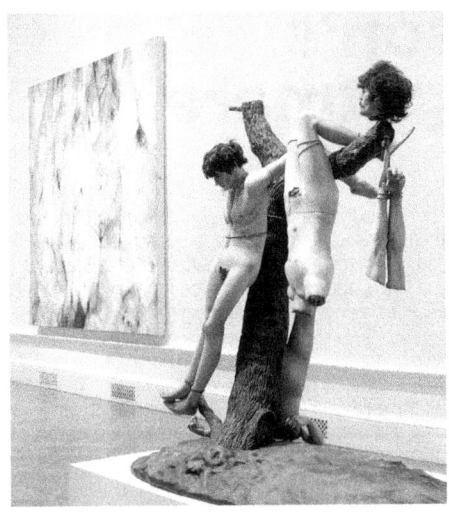

at a table laid out for four people. The plates and cutlery are bare and devoid of food except for several dead mice lying randomly amongst them. This darkness is even more pronounced and nightmarish in Morgan's more recent creations like *Carrion Call* (2009), in which a crumbling coffin bursts with hundreds of canary birds desperately struggling to get out through any holes or escape routes offered or *Pyric Victors*, in which a child's coffins bursts with hundreds of struggling and tormented birds in a scene worthy of any horror film.

It is in art's ability to shock and impress with an idea that the horror film can draw from. Art can be both elitist and off-putting, but it can also innovate and break boundaries, its practitioners forever seeking the shock of the new in order to impress, and as with film, they need to do so in order to keep their audience happy.

There are many parallels that one can draw, the not least of which being horrors increasing reliance on shock and special effects over ideas and content. Art's 'shock and awe' period was exciting, highly creative and at times brilliant. yet the art world has been forced to justify its pursuit of the visceral over the visual and artists expound on their creations in ways that have forced them to think through their ideas and justify the great offence their works sometimes cause. Telling the mother of a murdered child that "it is art" and dismissing her cries with a shrug of the shoulders just won't do and nor should it.

Conversely, the horror film in many ways has had a fairly easy ride in recent years, as blame culture has given way to lame culture, with apathy and inertia replacing our previous obsession with linking horror onscreen with real life events off-screen. Yet this reprieve has led in many ways to a period of horror inertia, with horror films becoming increasingly formulaic and clone-like, as ideas and creativity are usurped by a McDonald's 'churn them out' mentality. Perhaps it is time for the horror film industry to borrow a leaf from the art world and bring some genuine 'shock and awe' rather than just reproducing the same old pictures, albeit with a different frame again and again.

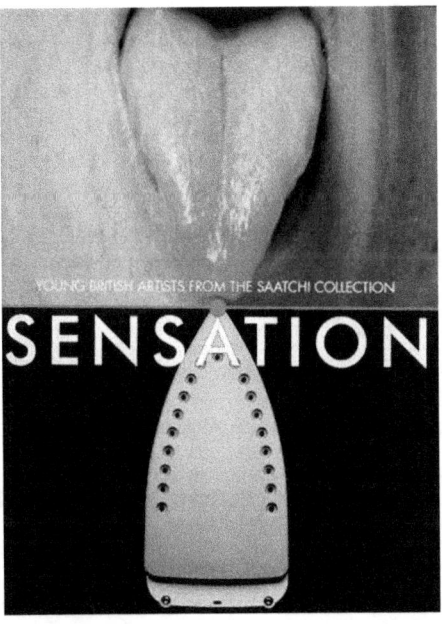

alan jefferson's galactic nightmare

Words: Daz Lawrence

There's no reason that the tag 'Outsider Music' shouldn't be looked upon with the same disdain that other lazy musical pigeonholes demand - an instruction to prepare, pre-judge and adjust your expectations does neither party any good. However, it would be churlish of me not to place this release in some kind of context, and this is about as far removed from the belching juggernaut of the music industry in the mid-Eighties as it's possible to imagine.

Alan Jefferson, an amateur musician from Hull, had a concept for an album comparable to Jeff Wayne's **War of the Worlds**. Suites of music and storytelling would combine to take the listener on a journey to unexplored pockets of the galaxy, a voyage of staggering depth and danger, one which would be immersive, thrilling and fantastic, in the true sense of the word. Alan would employ all the tools available to him; a mini-Moog, Hammond C3, guitar, reel-to-reel recording equipment and, most essential of all, his prowess as a singer and lyricist. Both concept and creation dictate that Alan was indeed an outsider, a visionary too brave for the mainstream, too determined to let even polite criticism deter him from his goal.

Galactic Nightmare took six years to make. I've written 'six' to ensure you don't think I've mis-typed a sensible number. Six years, and the fruits of his labours were made available to the masses on cassette via two portals, both magazines; **CU Amiga** (no longer with us) and **Future Music** (still extolling the virtues of electronic sound). The 86-minute epic came with a story file, should you struggle to keep up with proceedings, as well as a poster to stare at and contemplate your place in the universe, and reflect on whether this was necessarily the best £4.99 you'd ever spent. The gestation period had allowed Alan time to cover every minute detail of the release; the cover (also created by his own hand) declared it to be the product of Stargate Productions, the catalogue number of STAR1 pleasingly giving the impression this may only be the first of many releases...so long as you were comfortable with six year gaps between projects. Assurances were given as to the chromey qualities of the tape used, lest anyone think this is a project of mere folly.

Luckily, one person was forward-thinking enough to recognise the majestic scope of the album - Dave Robinson, a writer at **Future Music**. It wasn't until the next decade that he shared **Galactic Nightmare** with a friend, who in turn passed it onto the comedian and writer, Stewart Lee, who was equally smitten. Only last year did the album end up in the hands of Jonny Trunk, who, after contacting Alan (still at the same address in Hull listed on the advertisement), was able to release this in a more futuristic form (double vinyl). From the nugget of an idea to this review, 36 years have passed. How has it fared?

Firstly, let us quickly dispense with the 'plot' - after crash landing on the planet Zeon, Commander Bron, shorn of both his crew and passengers, ventures out into the wild unknown, first battling the Groth before becoming embroiled in a conflict between them and the Immortals, body harvesters ravaging their innocent prey. Frankly, that's plenty to be getting on with. Musically, the opening themes are endearingly creaky, hiccuping John Carpenter-lite melodies, which by 1986 would already have sounded as dated as the six years they had taken to appear, but have now taken on a somewhat timeless quality, the facelessness of the production and the not entirely perfectly-functioning instruments behaving in a way it would be impossible to adopt in any plagiaristic or ironic way. This is a man doing his absolute best with everything he has at his disposal.

Things take a turn for the stranger once the narration starts. Alan's quaintly gentle Yorkshire accent is not an attempt to replicate Richard Burton's florid tones - or maybe it is, which makes it even more magnificent - rather it is an amalgam of the spoken word intro to Spinal Tap's Stonehenge with the leisurely self-surprise of Ivor Cutler. As with the presentation of the cassette itself, Alan is at pains to give us every possible detail of the interstellar tale: the number of passengers on the craft; their injuries and prognosis; Bron's thoughts and observations, indeed every drop of Jefferson's mental juice is on display in one form or another.

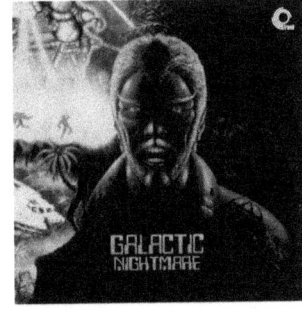

If the picture painted is of an idyll of individual genius, rest assured that there is also an abject lesson in the dangers of going it alone. **Galactic Nightmare** deafeningly screams for someone to shout, *"stop"*. Not in any negative way but to cut away a little of the descriptive web - less is more and all that. *"Having made a fire for heat and warmth"*, on the off-chance we're unfamiliar with fire, is a line typical of Alan's desperate desire to not only please but to finally get the whole project out of his system. Perhaps unintentionally, his storytelling is very similar to the pithy paragraphs of the **Fighting Fantasy** and **Choose Your Own Adventure** books that were rife at the time of release.

If the narration, though huge fun, is a little overdone, the musical backdrop is far more accomplished. The sounds of exotic flora and fauna are evoked with assorted bloops, squawks and pedalled burblings to great effect, belying the zero budget trappings and revealing Alan as a man of infinite patience and pride in his work. It veers a little from tense space drama to dry ice Kate Bush video largesse but we must accept this as further evidence of his genius.

His singing voice, first glimpsed on the beginning of side 2's **Old and Grey**, is a startling Bryan Ferry-esque drawl, an eyes-closed hymn in which he occasionally, some would say thrillingly, hits the correct notes. You find yourself willing him on like a proud parent at a school sports day, cheering on their offspring as they lurch with blood and tears squirting from their face towards the finishing line, regardless of the fact that everyone else finished ten minutes ago. Eventually, any slight atonality becomes completely common place, indeed, if you're foolish enough to put another album on afterwards, rather than immediately replaying this, any other music just sounds...wrong.

One other vocalist also gets an opportunity to shine, John Stoker, whose 'rock' vocals do slightly suggest repeated goosing when attempting the high notes, and Ken Worthington when on firmer ground. Neither of these should be taken as negatives, indeed no element of this release deserves anything less than palm-ruining applause. As the album progresses there are nods towards The Who's **Tommy**, maybe even a nudge and a wink too. It is true that some of the lyrics don't quite fit the melodies but who says they should?

AJ's Science Fantasy Musical, as the cassette cover proudly proclaims, is nothing less than magnificent. It could well be the case that not a single release in the 21st Century has taken longer to create, certainly none have come close to being as daring or ambitious. **Galactic Nightmare** is not a glorious failure, an ironic gem or a misguided triumph; it's real music from a real person, revealing the development of auto-tune and ProTools as the horror story they are. Caps doffed to the few who recognised AJ's talent and kept the release alive, as well as to Jonny for once again going where no man has gone before.

An expectant public eagerly awaits STAR2.

greetings from the salton sea

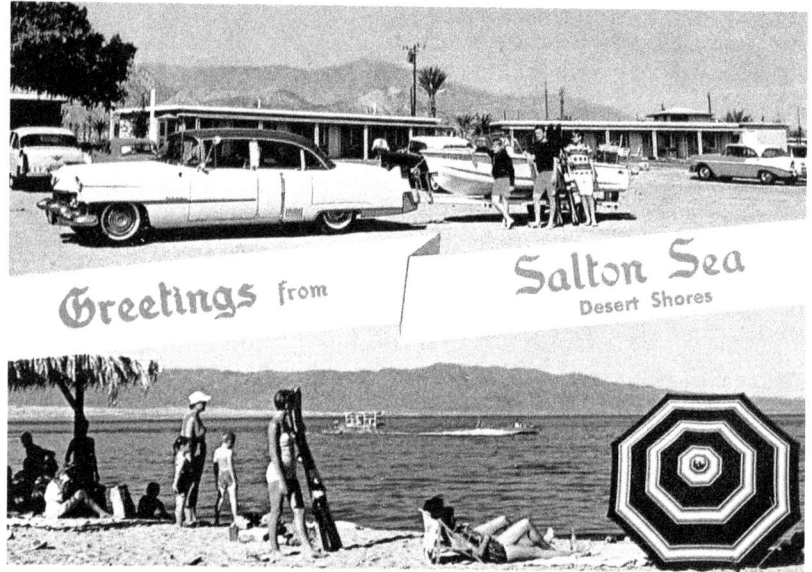

Words: Lucy Morrow
Photos: Gavin Morrow

In the Southernmost part of California is an expanse of stagnant water, thirty five miles long by fifteen miles wide. A by-product of the State's plan to re-direct the Colorado River through the previously dry valley for irrigation purposes in the early twentieth century, the Salton Sea shouldn't really be there at all. But there it is on the map; California's largest lake; lonely, decaying and in need of attention.

It didn't always look like this. In the 1950s, investors saw potential in this real-life desert oasis, and built several exclusive beach resorts on both sides of the sea. Their "miracle in the desert" thrived, attracting half a million visitors a year, before the cracks began to show. Within ten years, the desert heat, rising salt levels from the desert basin, toxic run-off from agricultural irrigation systems, and the introduction of Tilapia fish into a habitat where they could breed into the millions every year meant that, soon, the water was no longer the draw it once was, and summers brought beaches covered in stinking dead fish and debris. The holiday-makers left in droves, and the once-glamorous resorts were abandoned.

Our first encounter with the Salton Sea was a couple of days before Christmas 2012. We'd taken the scenic route through the Algodones Sand Dunes, stopped off at the small town of Brawley, and turned North to follow the coastal road on the Eastern Side of the sea. Glances from the car window would have one believe that this was a beautiful unspoiled area and a haven for wildlife. It wasn't until we found ourselves passing through the entrance to ex-resort Bombay Beach 40 miles later that we started to feel a strangeness in the air.

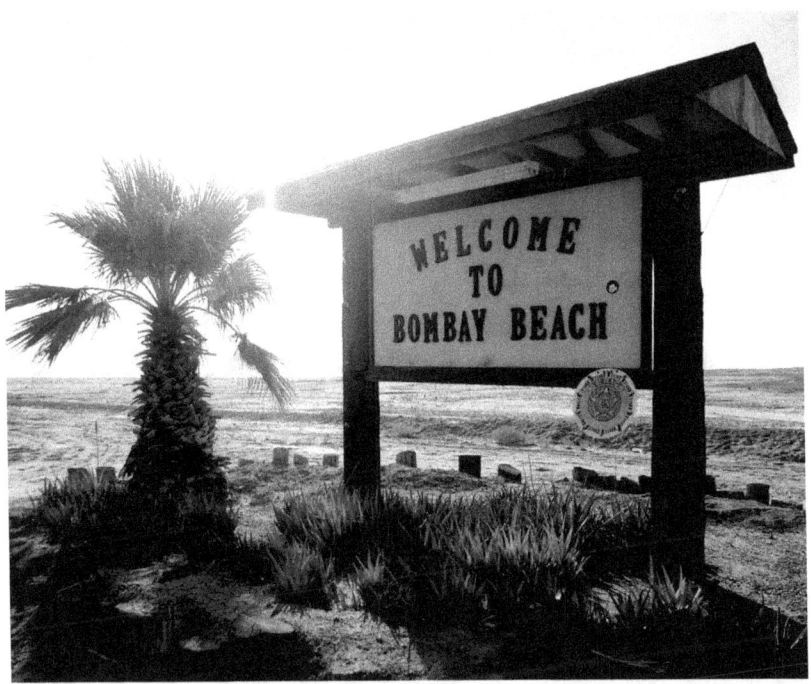

As we rolled over the cracked pavements into town, we began to realise that this wasn't quite the ghost town we'd imagined. But only just, by the grace of God. Dusty blocks of derelict trailers and smashed-up pre-fab buildings were peppered with the odd sign of life; individual well-kept yards with intact fences, decorated with Americana, and the occasional dog barking to keep out intruders. We also noticed the strange popularity of golf carts.

We drove very slowly, taking everything in. People actually *live* here, we thought to ourselves.

We reached the berm at the end of Avenue B - created to keep out the floods - and drove up the steep ramp to find what we'd been looking for.

To say it felt like we had arrived in some post-apocalyptical world is no exaggeration. The remains of buildings that once stood on the shoreline had been destroyed by years of weather, together with extreme salt and water damage. Barely anything remained. Anything near to the water was completely encrusted with a thick layer of corrosive salt, and as we started to explore the area, we began to realise that what had looked from a distance like white sand on the shore was actually a carpet of dead, desiccated fish, bones and scales.

After spending hours wandering up and down the beach taking photographs, we reluctantly returned to our car and made our way back into the town. As it was a little later in the day, there were a few more signs of life now; solitary golf carts trundling through the dust. We eyed them quizzically as we drove away. Later we learned that the golf cart is the preferred mode of transport for residents of Bombay Beach, simply because there is no gas station for over twenty miles.

The hot summer of 2013 was our second encounter with the Salton Sea, as we explored the West Coast. Rather more populated than the East Coast, there are still a few businesses

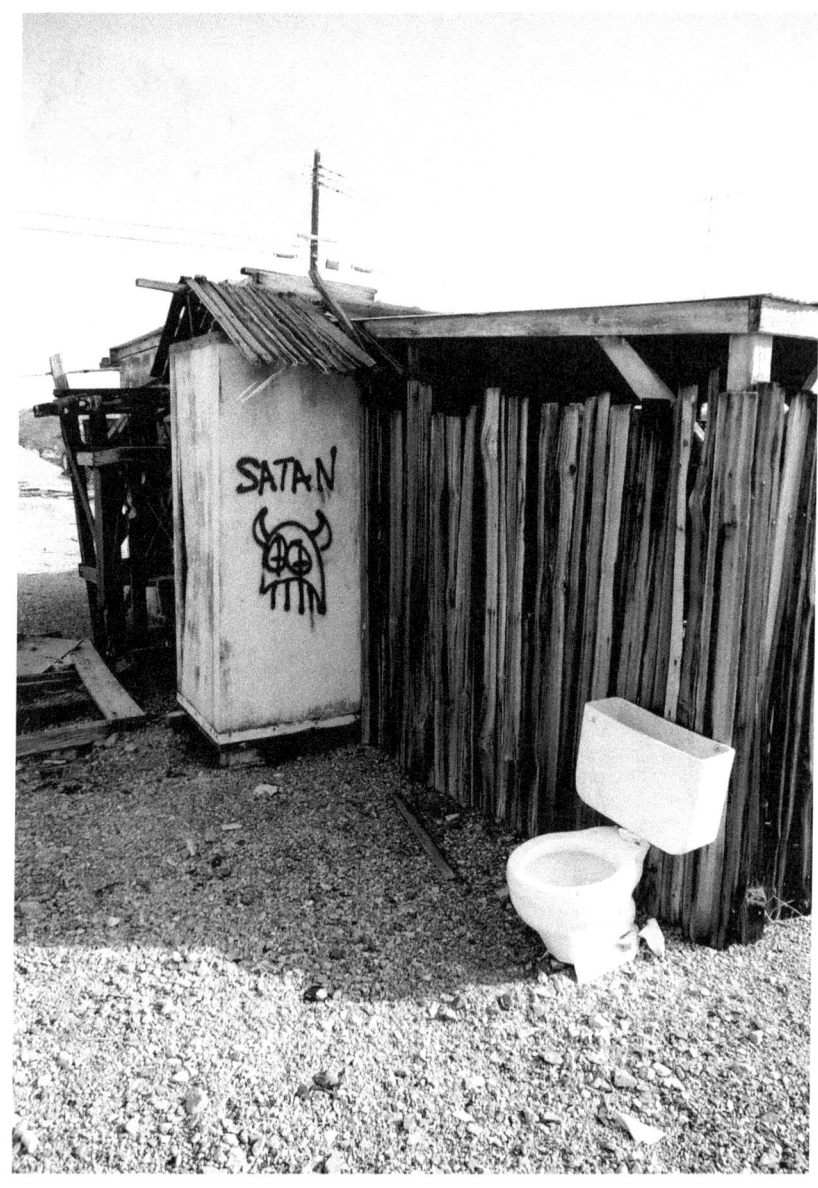

running in the several small towns here, including a lone guest house (Ray & Carol's Motel By the Sea - www.rayandcarolsmotel.com) and a couple of ramshackle grocery stores.

Although the towns on the West coast are obviously not what they were intended to be in the 1950s and '60s, and admittedly there are some parts of the towns that rival Bombay Beach with their post-apocalypse look, there also seems to be a sense of something up-and-coming about certain areas too. The growing town of Desert Shores, for example, now has a population of over a thousand people, and some of the newer properties really do give a sense of "Palm Springs by the Sea".

On our arrival in Salton Sea Beach, we decided once again to head straight for the shoreline. This time, the end of the road brought us to an inlet of florescent pink water, at which we stood quite transfixed for a while. Then we noticed an exuberant, shabbily dressed man with a huge smile walking towards us in the blazing sunshine with an outstretched hand.

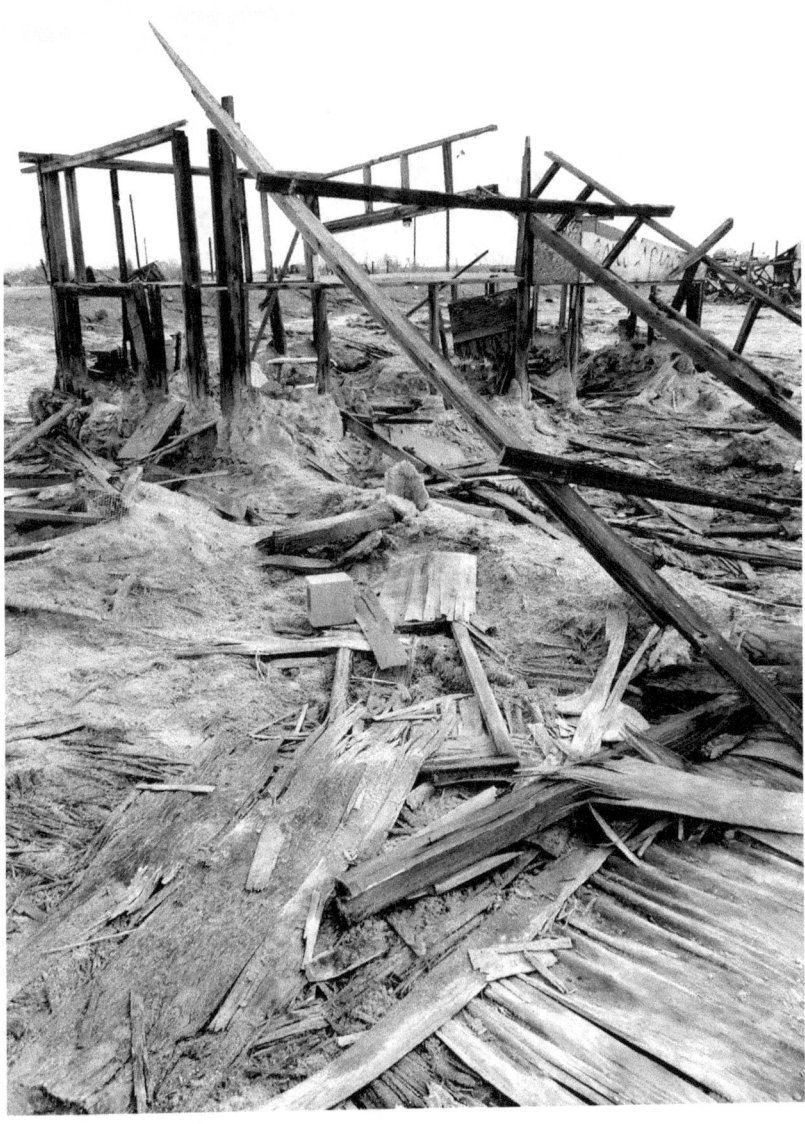

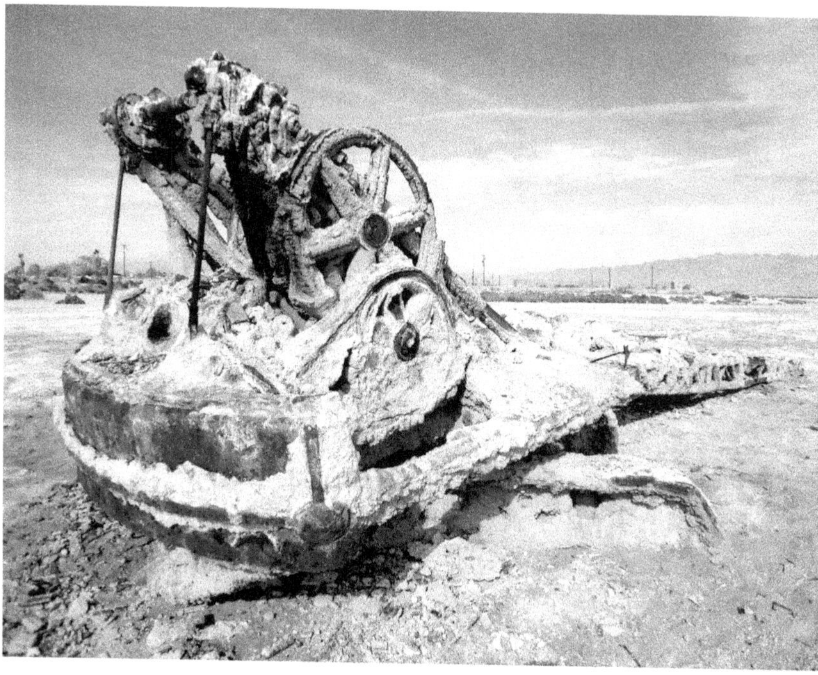

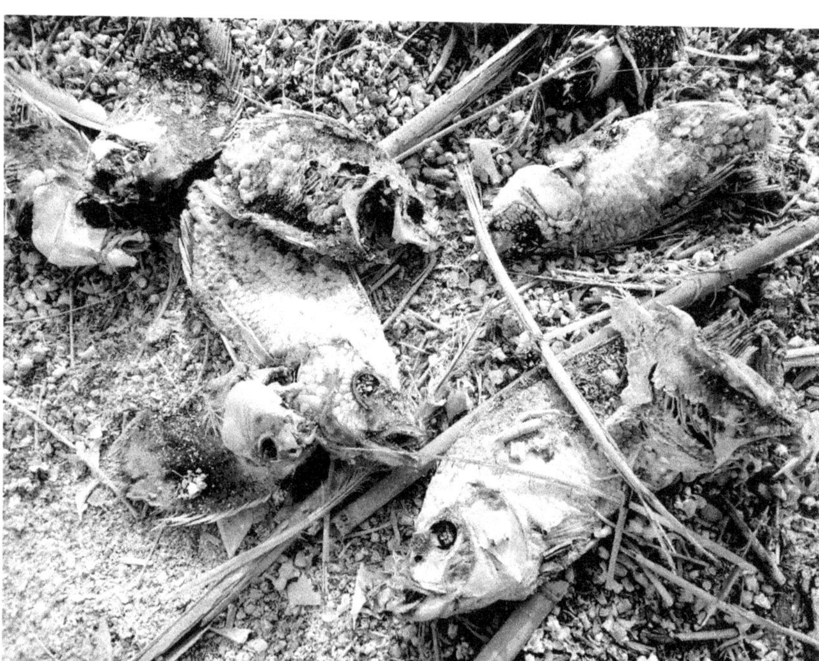

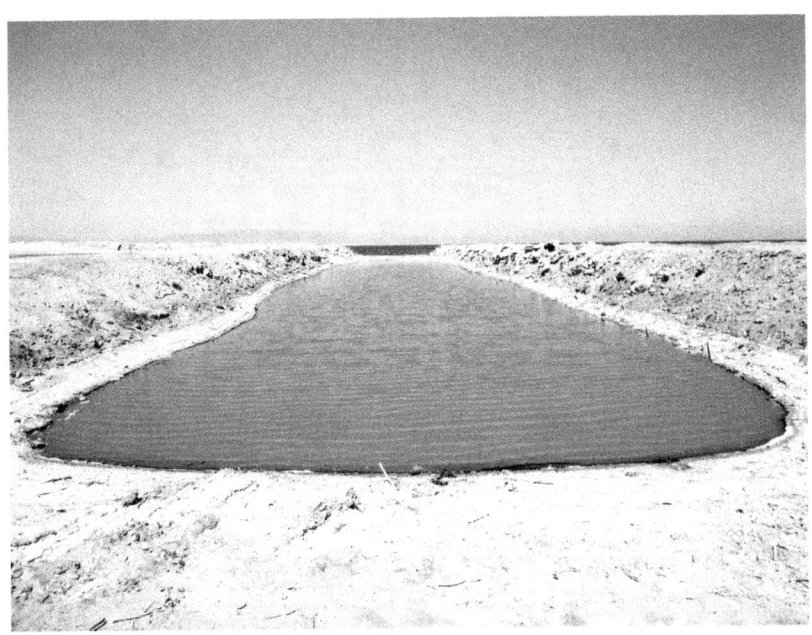

"Hello!" he called, "Don't worry, I'm not mad!"

I'll admit this did come as a relief. The man introduced himself and told us that he was originally from Florence, but now lived in Salton Sea Beach. He explained that the colour of the water before us was due to the high concentration of a certain type of algae that thrives in the high salt levels, and went on to tell us about some of the conservation efforts that have been attempted in the area, including one led by the late Sonny Bono. He then confided in us how the sea sometimes whispers secrets to him…

After saying our goodbyes to the Wild Man of Florence, we went off to explore the town. I should point out that the temperatures on this visit were significantly higher than on our December excursion. Now I've heard about people being "blinded by sweat" before, but never have I experienced this phenomenon until this day. Our relaxed exploration soon became a series of short guerrilla missions to take as many photographs as possible out in the sun before the heat made it impossible to see, and forced you to return to the car for air conditioned relief. But with photo-opportunities a-plenty, it had to be done.

Finally, when we could stand the heat nor the reek of rotten fish no more, we decided to cool ourselves down properly, and visited the grocery store in Salton Sea Beach Marina, where a group of elderly ladies and gentlemen wearing baseball caps sat smoking cigars and playing poker in the corner by the refrigerators.

As we left the Salton Sea that day, it was as reluctantly as when our first visit ended. But we knew that we would return.

In fact, if you check back in forty years' time, I fully intend that you'll find our golf carts parked outside the Salton Sea Marina Grocery Store, and we'll be inside playing poker with a man from Florence who talks to the sea.

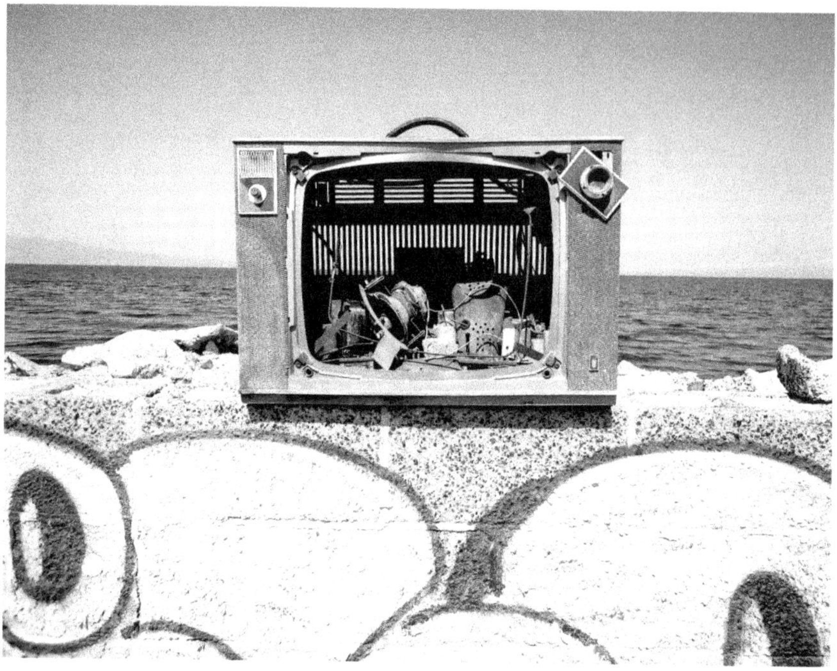

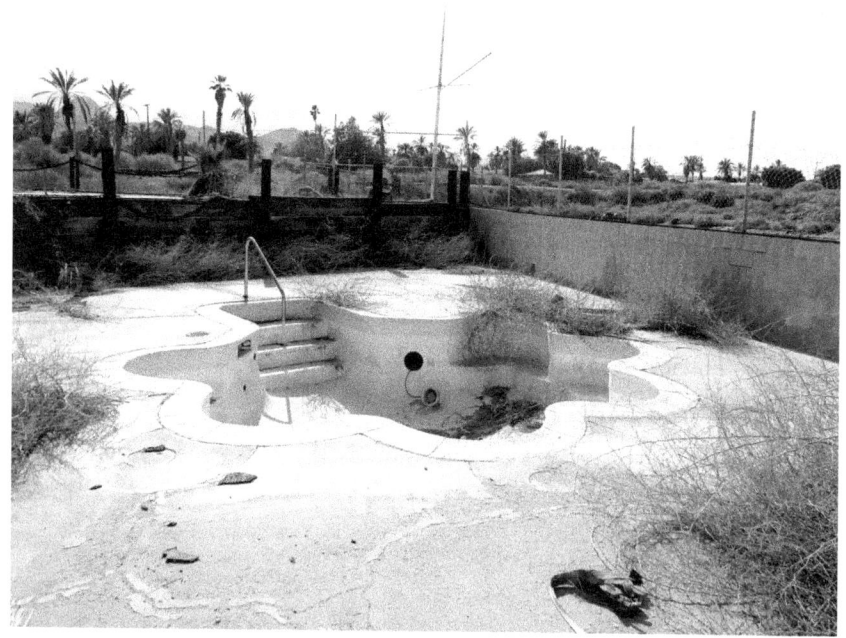

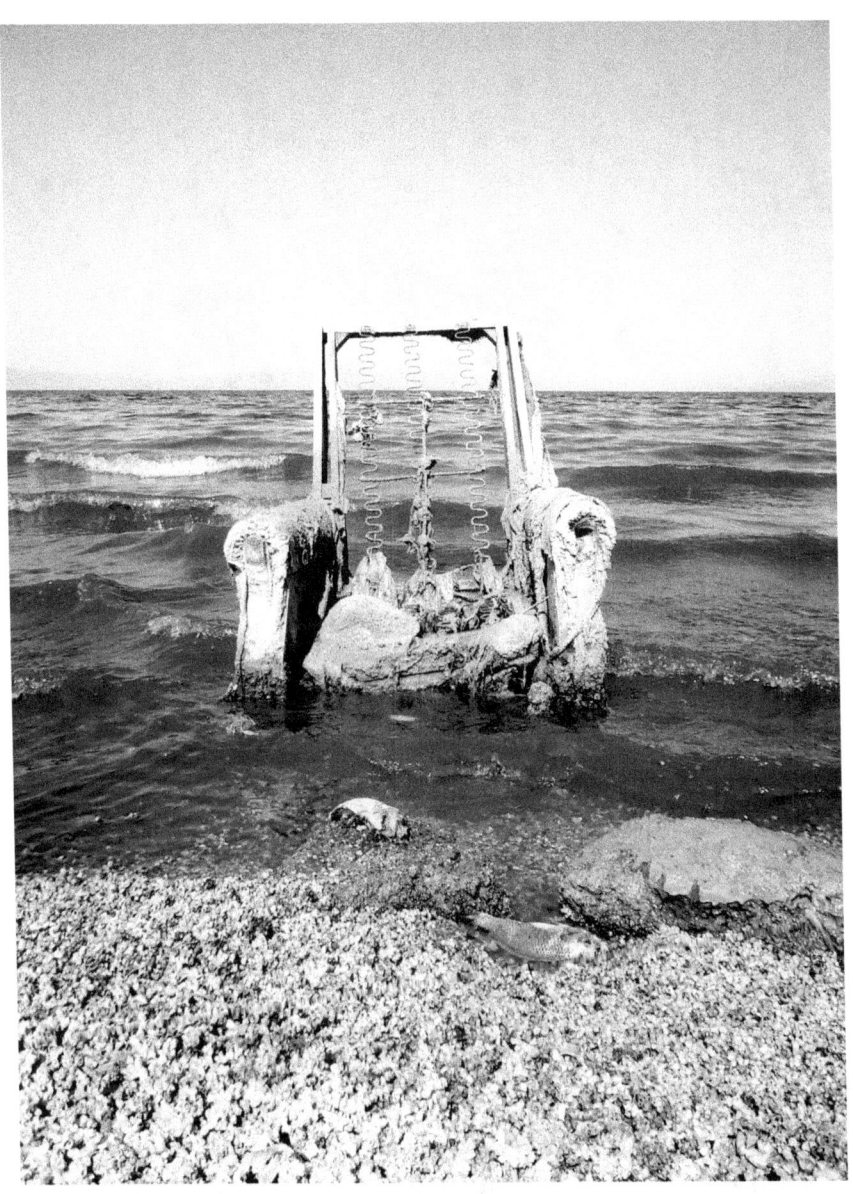

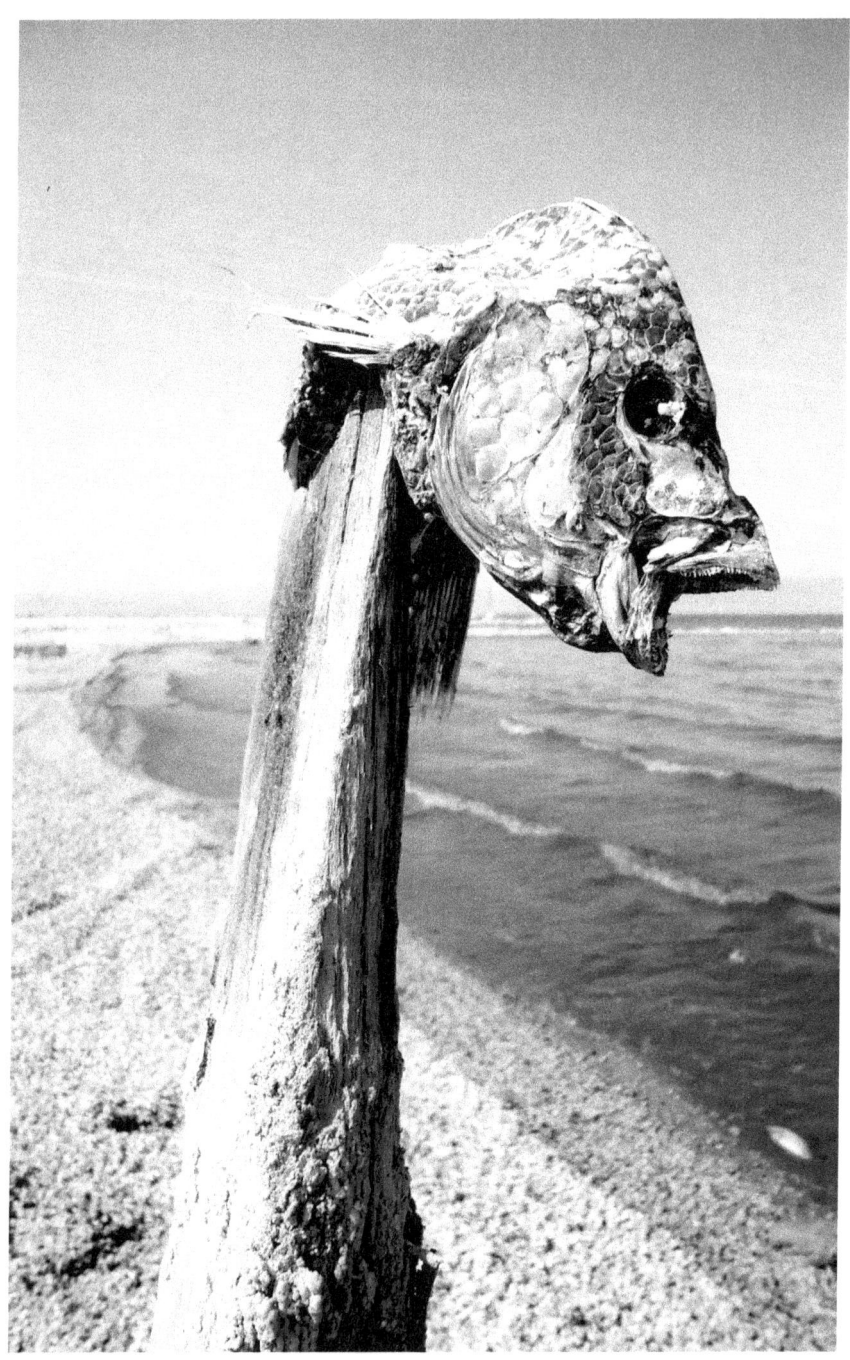

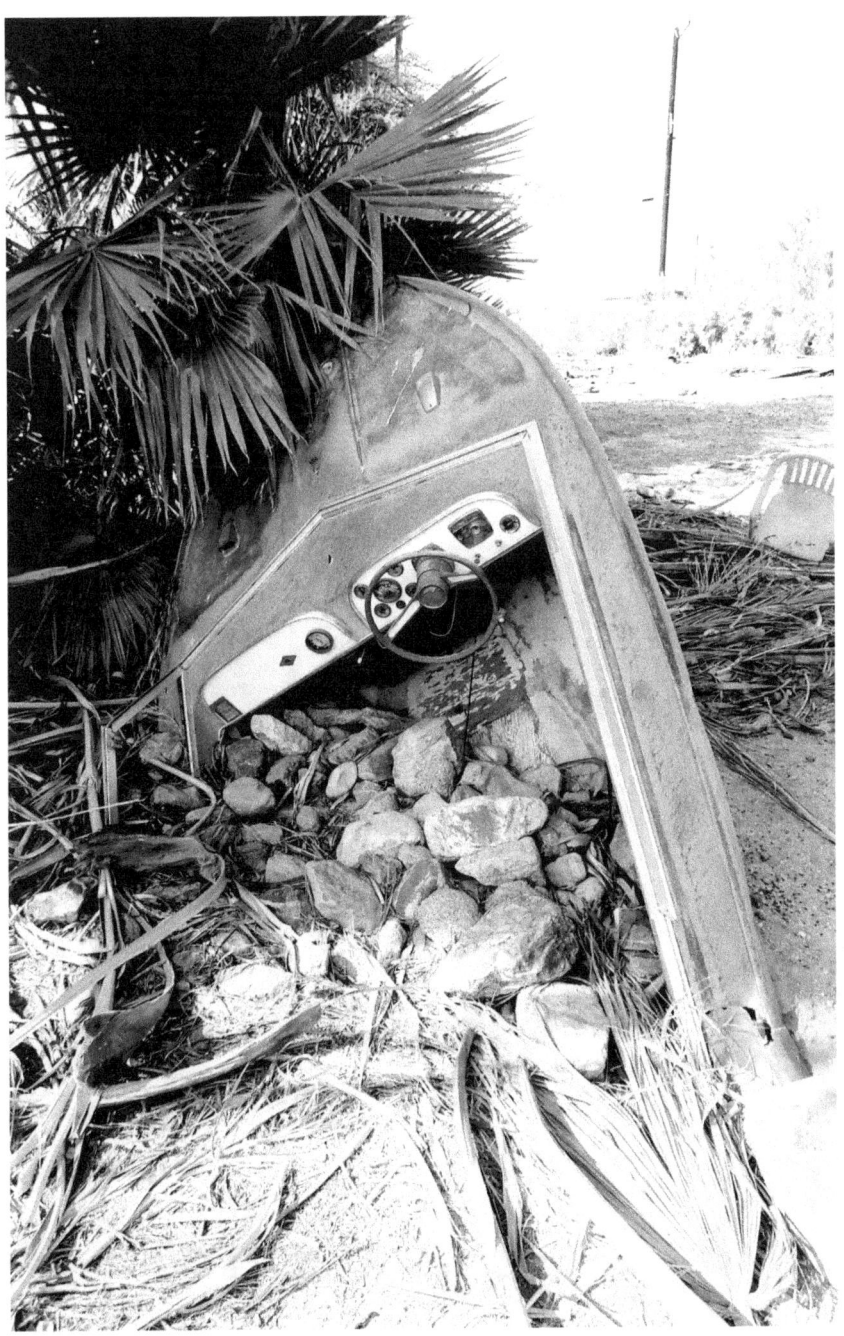

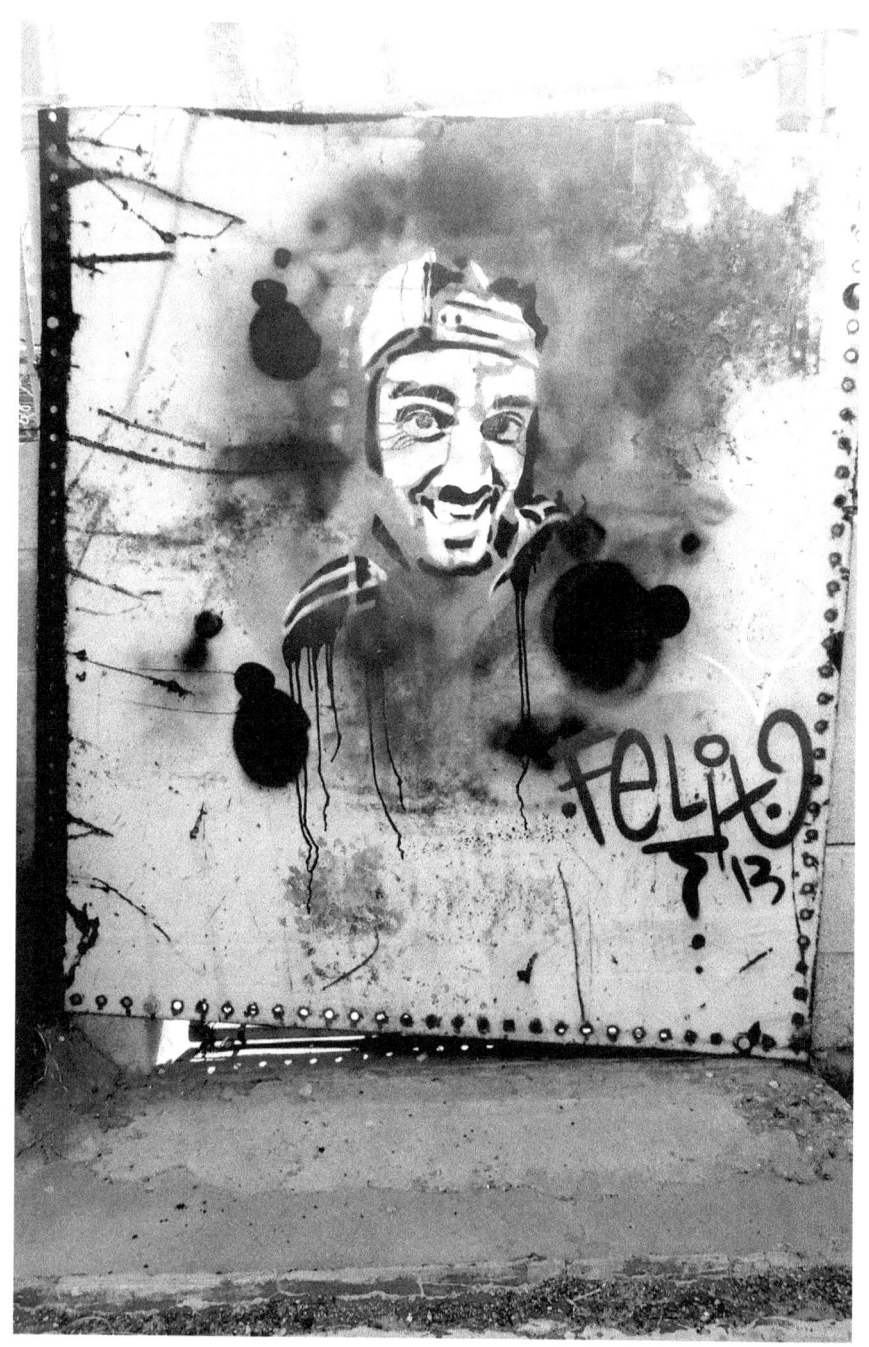

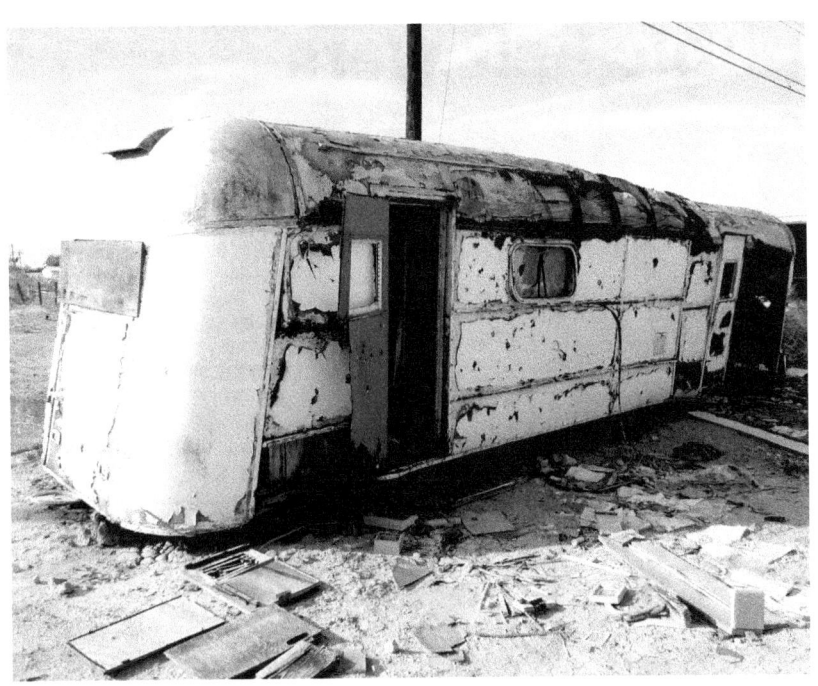

We recommend the 2004 documentary **Plagues and Pleasures at the Salton Sea** (Dir. Chris Metzler & Jeff Springer), narrated by John Waters.

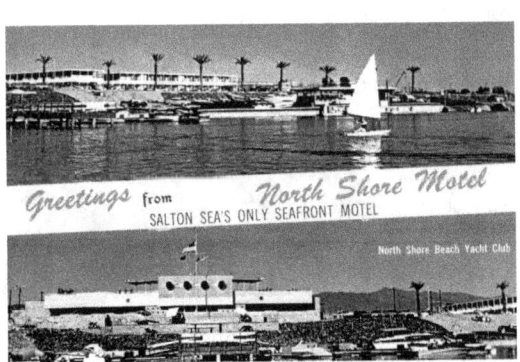

pubic hair wars

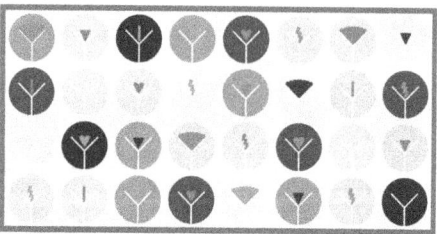

Words: David Flint

You can always tell when various groups are trying to flag something up as 'a cause for concern'. Both the right and the left have got it down to a fine art now – a series of seemingly unconnected articles in different newspapers, websites and blogs, suddenly drawing attention to something that has been going on for years without concern, and hyping it into an issue that suddenly, urgently needs to be dealt with. Be it internet porn, violent video games, happy hour in pubs, fast food or whatever social issue newspaper hacks and editors have decided is Unacceptable, often egged on in the background by assorted pressure groups that they might share socio-political ideals with.

Over the last couple of years, I've seen several articles cropping up about pubic hair – or, more accurately, the removal of it. Paranoia about pubes has become a bit of an obsession for the extremist divisions of the right and the left, it seems, with regular bursts of outrage from assorted hacks, furious that people are refusing to do as they are told with their own bodies. It's been a bête-noire for the **Guardian**'s regularly deranged *Comment Is Free* columnists for a while of course, but we've also had the BBC, **The Independent** and others climbing on the bandwagon that might have normally been the preserve of the more irate and controlling side of the Radical Feminist movement.

One of the first recent examples of journalists attempting to make a mountain out of a molehill came couple of years ago, when **Independent** columnist Louisa Saunders stated (in a piece stridently called **The Politics of Pubic Hair**) that *"shaved genitals have somehow become the new normal for an entire generation of women. Surely it's time we asked why."* One might counter that surely it's none of your damned business what women - or men, for that matter - choose to do with their own bodies. But of course, the entire *raison d'etre* of newspaper columnists – particularly virtue-signalling social justice columnists - is to make a big deal about things that really don't matter and to turn the personal into the political. And like a dog with a bone, the **Independent** quickly ran another three pieces that discuss the 'issue', directly or otherwise, since. And to think some people wonder why they went out of print.

The BBC has also weighed in on their website. Well, of course they have – the is the organisation that soberly reported recently on the pressing issue of 'thin privilege', a concept that only exists in the fevered imaginations of middle class acadumbics. The BBC report was a hysterical warning about the medical dangers and infections that could result from *"seeking a well-groomed bikini line"*, as they delicately put it, though the scare story was somewhat undermined by the statement

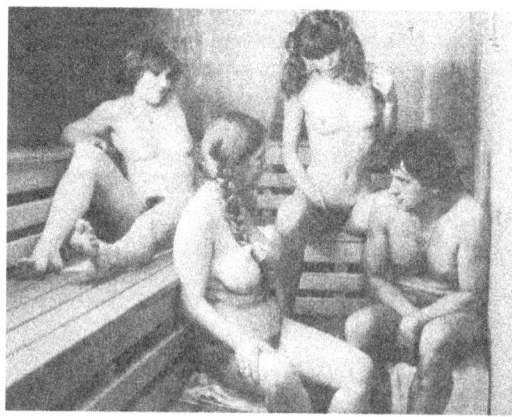

that pox virus molluscum contagiosum *"usually clears up on its own and does not cause any symptoms other than raised red spots."* Not exactly a massive cause for concern, then. But that didn't stop the **Guardian** (again, of course) from running a piece fretting that (according to a YouGov study) 26% of people who remove their pubic hair had reported injures. Aside from the fact that 26% would be (rightly) seen as a small minority if the stats added up to something that the **Guardian** approves of, it's worth noting that 61% of those injuries were cuts – which men routinely experience while shaving their faces, which did not require medical attention and were certainly not life-threatening. Some might suggest that this is a storm in a teacup (or at least a G-string).

When not fretting about the insignificant health issues of pubic hair removal, these campaigners (and that's what they are, make no mistake) are desperately crowing that *"pubic hair is back in fashion"*. You can always tell when a movement is desperately trying to posit something as a trend, because the same claims turn up year after year, with little evidence that anyone in the real world is taking notice. The **Independent** claimed that the tide had turned in 2017; in 2018, both the **Guardian** and **Vogue** – who's teen division, lest we forget, is currently the social justice anti-capitalist bible when not gushing over high-end fashion and vacuum-minded celebrities – also declared that pubes were back. These reports smack more of wishful thinking and desperate attempts at social engineering than any actual movement. I've no doubt that the sheer relentless attacks on shaving and the fatuous linking with porn has persuaded some of the Woke to grow out their bushes for political reasons, but outside the college campuses and the slactivist movements, I suspect people are carrying on much as they did before.

Pubic hair does, of course, exist for a reason, as anti-shavers love to point out. But then so does the rest of our hair, and no-one seems overly worked up about people shaving their heads or their armpits (OK, the more extreme feminists also get worked up about armpit hair). So far, claims of what shaving could do in terms of infection haven't been followed with any actual evidence of what it has done.

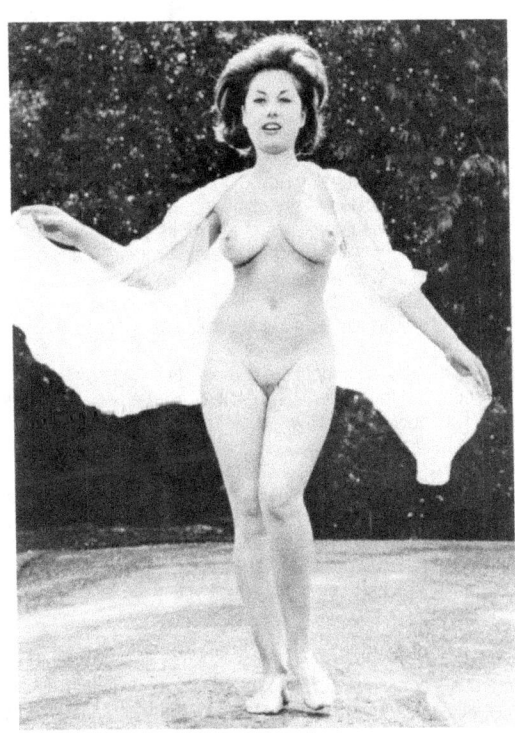

What goes without saying is that none of the writers 'debating' pubic shaving are claiming that it is a good thing. None of them seem to think that it is a personal choice that has nothing to do with them either. No, this is a Cause For Concern. It's something that people are not really doing through choice, but are instead being manipulated into thinking is acceptable by dubious outside forces. Like 'beach-ready' bodies and cosmetic surgery, pubic shaving is seen as a patriarchal imposition – male advertisers dictating to women how they should look. To paraphrase a Tory MP in the time of the Video Nasties, the public have made their choice but the public are wrong. Angry newspaper columnists know best, and it's apparently perfectly fine for *them* to tell you how to look – after all, they are doing it for the right reasons. The idea that they, as people rejecting the choices of what they admit is the majority, are the ones who are out of step with the norm and therefore in the wrong – well, that's just silly.

It is, of course, porn that is usually blamed for the trend. It's easy to understand why. Not only do these sort of writers disapprove of porn in general to begin with, but it's within the adult industry that the trend is most obvious. After all, most of us don't tend to see that many strangers naked from day to day, but porn allows us to intimately examine the newly hairless private parts of hundreds of performers. It must, therefore, be the fault of porn – another malicious influence on our soft-headed young people who watch this filth and think this is how people are supposed to look.

The problem with this theory is that it's one expounded by people with little actual experience of porn. As someone who has written about adult movies since the 1980s, and worked within the industry for some time, I can assure you that the theorists have got the chicken and egg situation backwards. Porn didn't start this trend, it simply followed it. I certainly remember that the gradual move towards the 'shaven haven' (as a once-specialist magazine was titled) - from basic trimming to landing strips to zero tolerance – was something I saw in real life a while long before it became the norm in porn. My own experience is that all this began in the 1990s, hitting the fetish clubbers and my own partners long before it became the norm in porn. By the end of the decade, a hairless genital area wasn't an unusual sight.*

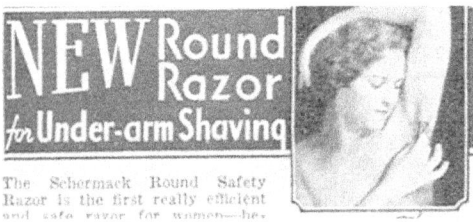

The rise in body grooming is, in fact, more directly connected to the rise in body art. It's not unreasonable to think that a generation that increasingly sees tattooing and piercing as normal will want more control over the visual aesthetic of their body in general. If you have piercings, then you've already made that step to prettifying and emphasising that (usually hidden) part of the body and you're probably not going to be inclined to hide them under a thatch of hair. If you are tattooed, then likewise you are turning your body into a work of art – it's unsurprising then that you might want that canvas to look its best. For many (though certainly not all) people, that means smooth skin and no body hair. Of course, many of the people who are upset by pubic shaving are also upset by genital or nipple piercings, though they are often more reluctant to express that disapproval because doing so reveals their real problem – that the ostentatious display of/calling attention to the genitals is unacceptably immodest and indecent.

What's also curious about the complaints is that no one seems to say what is acceptable. Are we supposed to let everything grow au naturel, or is some trimming of the foliage acceptable? And if so, how much? At what point does body grooming cross the line into unacceptability? If we are being told what to do with our own bodies, then surely we need full disclosure.

Saunders comments that she sees this as a feminist issue, and to a degree, she's right. Though it's certainly not a mainstream feminist issue. As far as I'm aware, most feminists see a woman's right over her own body as fundamental, and rightly so. I've known several women who trimmed or completely shaved their pubes, and if you suggested to them that they were bad feminists, they'd probably punch you in the face. And you'd probably deserve it.

But there are the extremists in any movement who view any variation from their own narrow orthodoxy as heresy. Given that it was a badge of honour for the extreme RadFems who rose to prominence in the 1980s to reject armpit and leg shaving, along with make-up and styled hair, as pandering the male gaze and a media-created definition of 'beauty' - as was their right, of course - so pubic epilation is bound to have the same implications. Though of course, the 'let it grow' ethos was roundly rejected by - at least - 90% of women at the time and it must be frustrating to see that the situation has, if anything, become 'worse'.

The idea that modern women might not toe the party line – that they might actually exercise their individual freedom of choice instead of switching from one form of oppression to another – is one that they seem find hard to stomach. Surely no woman would reject these dictates by choice? And so we are told that the trend is because of the malicious influence of internet porn, of male demands or – most idiotically – because of some paedophile fantasy that wants to turn women into hairless child-women (though quite how this fits with that other porn staple, the boob job, is never quite explained). After all, the other explanation - that these women, perfectly capable of thinking for themselves and making their own choices, have simply decided that they find the shaven look more aesthetically (and possibly sexually) pleasing – is unpalatable.

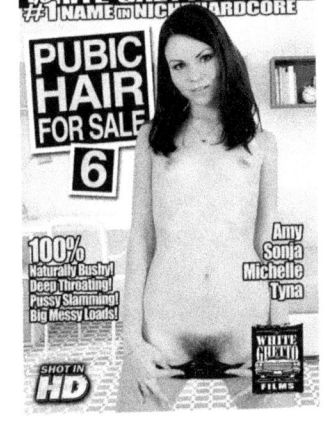

On the Right, pubic waxing is equally distressing. Not only is it related to the evil porn merchants in the minds of religious and moralistic zealots, but it also seems an ostentatious display – an attempt to bring the previous hidden and dirty female genitalia into the open, possibly even drawing attention to it. My God, not only are women shaving their pubes, but they can even buy 'vajazzling' kits in Poundland! No matter that classical images of Adam and Eve are hairless – the removal of pubic hair is seen as nothing more than a brazen display of sexuality and wantonness. After all, they will argue, why prettify your privates unless you intend to make them public? Another group who shout loudly but actually have little public support, the religious Right are continually mortified that, despite their best efforts, people are still having, and enjoying sex. They are, at least, more open in their fear of sexuality, but their arguments are no less fatuous. No one is stopping the religious from loathing their genitalia, but that does not give them the right to dictate what others do with theirs. But as they know - control what someone can do with their own genitals and you control their entire sexuality. And then you control them. No wonder they focus their attention on women.

But of course it's not just women who prefer the hairless look. Look at any media image of a hunky man with his shirt off and you won't see a single hair on their body. No male model is going to get work with a hirsute torso. In fact, hairy chests have become associated with the 1970s, but that isn't because there has been a sudden genetic shift in the last few decades. Men are not suddenly growing up devoid of hair. Chest shaving and the 'back, sack and crack' trend suggest that men too are falling for the depilated fashion, though I don't recall anyone suggesting that they are removing chest hair because women want to see them as children. Are they too pressured by porn? Or is it simply that a generation of men, like women, have seen the groomed look and decided that they like it?

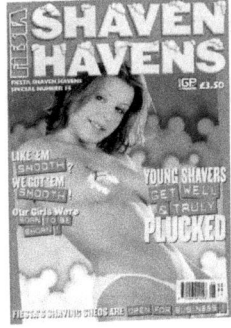

In the end, all this gnashing of teeth is really just a sign of frustration. Frustration that, despite all the newspaper columns, the tweeting and the hand wringing, most people are continuing to think for themselves and to behave accordingly. How awful it must be to know better than everyone else, only for them to ignore your wise words and make their own decisions. And for all the anger, what the hell can they actually do about it? Ban razors, waxing and body trimmers? Reclassify any image of

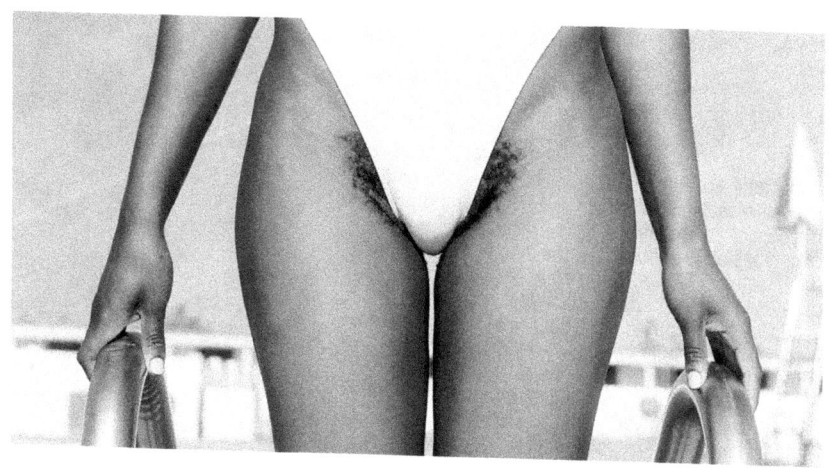

a hairless vagina as child porn? I suspect some people would like to do both, but in the real world, it's not going to happen.

And despite what the media is currently trying to tell us – more in a desperate attempt at social engineering or perhaps, as with so many other 'trends', simply the belief that what their own narrow social group does and thinks somehow reflects the broader sociality – there is no real evidence that public shaving is falling out of fashion. Angry Social Justice Warriors, strident feminists and attention freaks might be publicly and noisily bucking the trend, but that hardly puts them in the ascendency. The desire for personal grooming doesn't seem to be going anywhere, and there is no evidence of waxing salons all suddenly going out of business across the country.

Personally, I don't give a damn what someone chooses to do with / to their own body. I have my preferences, of course, but my opinion on the matter is nothing more than that – a personal one. If you want to be as hairy as a werewolf, that's fine; if you prefer to be as smooth as a billiard ball, that's fine too. It's really none of my business. And it's none of anyone else's either. Leave people to do what they want to their pubic hair – grow it, shave it, sculpt it, dye it or use it as a work of art or political expression – it really doesn't matter. Whatever makes you feel happy. Either way, unlike most body modification, it's not permanent or invasive – if you change your mind either way, it's easily 'fixed' - and despite attempts to claim otherwise, clearly isn't causing a public (or pubic) health epidemic. Unlike the shrill and desperate columnists, I really don't think that it's an issue worth getting worked up over.

* Of course, the hairless look was also common – in fact, legally essential – in 1960s nude photography, though no-one seems to be suggesting that it led to a spate of copycat trimming.

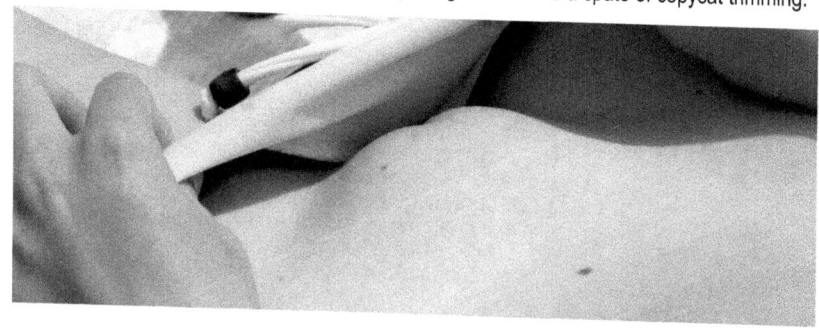

the lost classics of rock
abruptum - evil genius

words: Darius Drewe

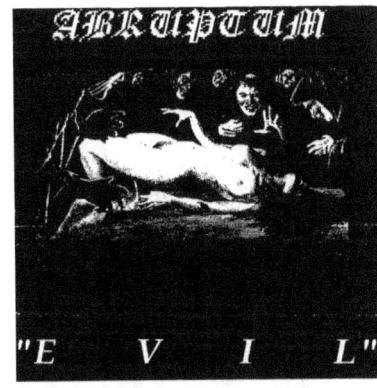

"The audial essence of pure black evil" is how Euronymous once described this Swedish blackened-doom project, and though the late Mayhem guitarist could be a bit of a twunt at times (well, a lot of one, to be honest) I'm pretty much behind him in this particular assessment. While I'd have jumped at the chance to see Mayhem with Dead on vocals, or the original Misfits lineup, the very thought of ever setting foot near this bunch still fills me with dread even today...

Led by the man who called himself IT (though his family called him Tony Sarkka) and still in existence - albeit as an ambient outfit - two whole decades after his departure from the metal scene altogether, Abruptum were, if played to the uninitiated, the kind of band who would have easily confirmed every parent's misconception of heavy metal as tuneless, dirge-like, devil-worshipping noise. The difference was, they set out to do that from the start, going one better than their Norwegian, French and American black metal contemporaries by eschewing any form of structured finesse, melody or even riffage in their recordings.

Indeed, the only vaguely fathomable parts of tracks- one hesitates to call them 'songs'- like **Honores Vultus Mutares Ex Aeris Campi, Feci Factum Sanguine Gladios Made Fieri Factus** and the impossibly sibilant **Animum, Mentem Alcis Juventutem Largitionibus, Hostes Ad Dimicandum, Commotis Exita Sacris Thyias** are IT's slow, lumbering guitar chords and drums, so lugubrious they make Swans sound like Cardiacs by comparison: elsewhere, the vocals of frontman All are mere screams, whispers and groans, allegedly caused by (although this remains unconfirmed) the other band members' tendency to cut him (and each other) during recording. I only hope they cleaned up after themselves, otherwise they might have invalidated their deposits (oo er Missus).

Following the direction of umpteen death threats (not helped by his association with Euronymous and Helvete) against both himself and his family, IT left first the band, then metal altogether: guitarist 'Evil' (aka Morgan Hakunsson of Marduk) has continued their work in a purely electronic vein since, but it's this release - consisting of the band's first three demos plus one bonus track - that still chills the spine nearly three decades on. Sarkka, also the founder of Sweden's True Satanic Horde, died of unspecified causes in 2017: as with most musicians within such fraternities, the truth, once revealed, could transpire to be either morbidly fascinating or prosaically dull. My money's on the latter.

yes... no... die!
the magical myth and tedious truth about ouija boards

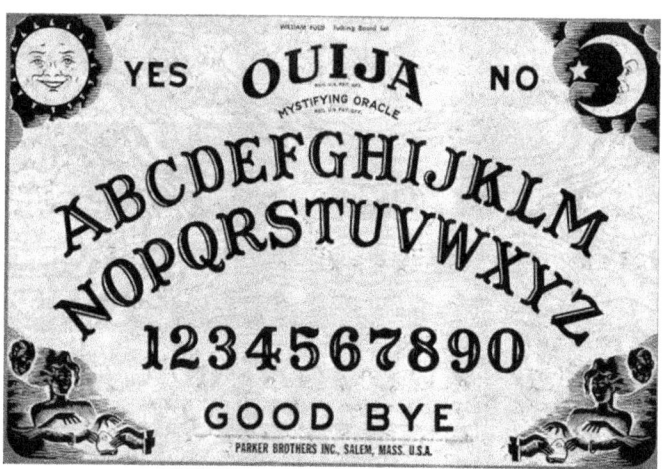

Words:
Daz Lawrence

There are essentially three things required to contact the dead: One, a dead person; Two, a living person to whom they are acquainted (or would like to be); Three, a very open mind. Of course, over the years tools have been introduced to help facilitate this communication, allowing both highly-tuned mediums and amateur inquisitors to speak to those in the realm beyond. Perhaps the most famous of these, despite being one of the most basic, is the Ouija board.

The Ouija, also known as a spirit board or talking board, is a flat board marked with the letters of the alphabet, the numbers 0–9, the words *"yes"*, *"no"*, *"hello"* (occasionally), and *"goodbye"*, along with various symbols and graphics. It uses a planchette (a small heart-shaped piece of wood or plastic) as a movable indicator to facilitate the communication of the spirit's message by spelling it out on the board during a séance. Participants place their fingers on the planchette, and it is moved about the board to spell out words, seemingly by a force other than the participants. 'Ouija' has become a trademark that is often used generically to refer to any talking board.

Early references to the automatic writing method used in the Ouija board is found in China around 1100 AD, in historical documents of the Song Dynasty. The method was known as fuji 'planchette writing'. The use of planchette writing as an ostensible means of contacting the dead and the spirit-world continued, and, albeit under special rituals and supervisions, was a central practice of the Quanzhen School, until it was forbidden by the Qing Dynasty. Several entire scriptures of the Daozang are supposedly works of automatic planchette writing. Similar methods of mediumistic spirit writing have been practiced in ancient India, Greece, Rome, and medieval Europe.

During the late 19th century, planchettes were widely sold as a novelty. Businessman Elijah Bond had the idea to patent a planchette sold with a board on which the alphabet was printed.

The patentees filed on May 28, 1890 for patent protection and thus is credited with the invention of the Ouija board. Bond was an attorney and was an inventor of other objects in addition to this device, including a steam boiler (not to be used for contacting the dead). Bond's self-produced board was named 'nirvana' and featured a swastika as a logo, well before the Nazis appropriated the religious symbol, and was launched on July 1st 1890.

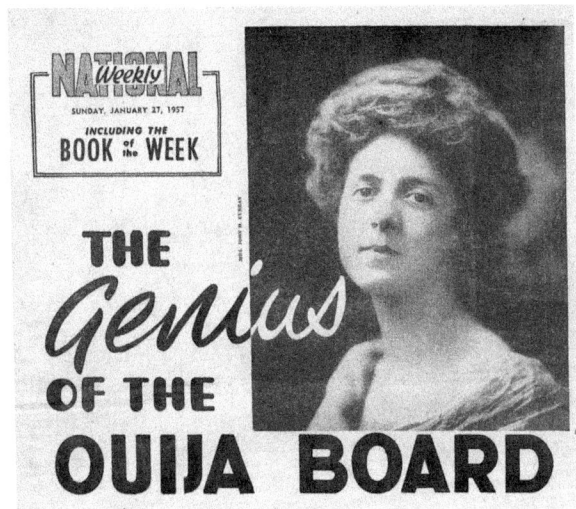

An employee of Elijah Bond, William Fuld took over the talking board production and in 1901, he started production of his own boards under the name 'Ouija'. Charles Kennard (founder of the Kennard Novelty Company that manufactured Fuld's talking boards and where Fuld had worked as a varnisher) claimed he learned the name 'Ouija' from using the board and that it was an ancient Egyptian word meaning 'good luck'. When Fuld took over production of the boards, he popularised the more widely accepted etymology: that the name came from a combination of the French and German words for 'yes'.

The Fuld name would become synonymous with the Ouija board, as Fuld reinvented its history, claiming that he himself had invented it. Fuld sued many companies over the 'Ouija' name and concept right up until his death in 1927. In 1966, Fuld's estate sold the entire business to Parker Brothers, which was sold to Hasbro in 1991, and which continues to hold all trademarks and patents. About ten brands of talking boards are sold today under various names – all are Ouija boards in every sense but the legal one.

The Ouija board was regarded as an innocent parlour game unrelated to the occult, until American Spiritualist Pearl Curran popularised its use as a divining tool during World War 1. Since then, it has been inextricably connected to the supernatural. Some mainstream Christian denominations have *"warned against using Ouija boards"*, holding that they can lead to demonic possession. Occultists, on the other hand, are divided on the issue, with some saying that it can be a positive transformation; others rehash the warnings of many Christians and caution *"inexperienced users"* against it.

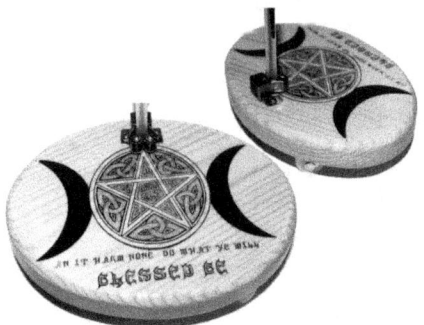

Most religious criticism of the Ouija board has come from Christians, primarily Roman Catholics and evangelicals in the United States. Catholic Answers, a Christian apologetics organisation, states that *"The Ouija board is far from harmless, as it is a form of divination (seeking information from supernatural sources). The fact of the matter is, the Ouija board really does work, and the*

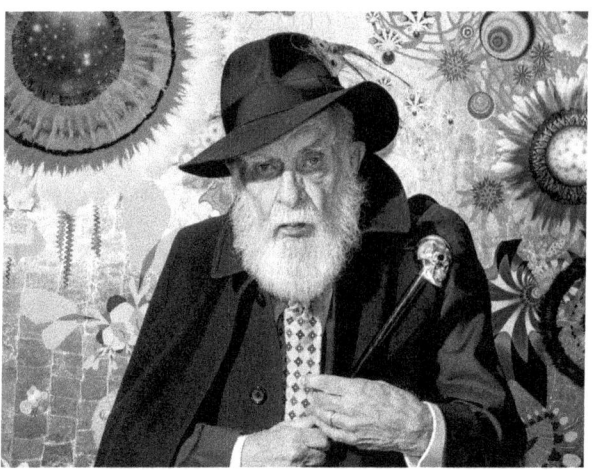
James Randi

only 'spirits' that will be contacted through it are evil ones."

In 2001, Ouija boards were burned in Alamogordo, New Mexico by fundamentalist groups alongside **Harry Potter** books (!) as *"symbols of witchcraft."* Religious criticism has also expressed beliefs that the Ouija board reveals information that should only be in God's hands, and thus it is a tool of Satan. A spokesperson for Human Life International described the boards as a portal to talk to spirits and called for Hasbro to be prohibited from marketing them. Bishops in Micronesia called for the boards to be banned and warned congregations that they were talking to demons and devils when using the boards.

Paranormal and supernatural beliefs associated with Ouija have been heavily criticised by the scientific community, since they are characterised as pseudoscience. The action of the board can be parsimoniously explained by unconscious movements of those controlling the pointer, a psychophysiological phenomenon known as the 'ideomotor effect'.

Various studies have been produced, recreating the effects of the Ouija board in the lab and showing that, under laboratory conditions, the subjects were moving the planchette involuntarily. Sceptics have described Ouija board users as 'operators'. Some critics noted that the messages ostensibly spelled out by spirits were similar to whatever was going through the minds of the subjects. According to Professor of neurology Terence Hines in his book **Pseudoscience and the Paranormal** (2003):

"The planchette is guided by unconscious muscular exertions like those responsible for table movement. Nonetheless, in both cases, the illusion that the object (table or planchette) is moving under its own control is often extremely powerful and sufficient to convince many people that spirits are truly at work... The unconscious muscle movements responsible for the moving tables and Ouija board phenomena seen at seances are examples of a class of phenomena due to what psychologists call a dissociative state. A dissociative state is one in which consciousness is somehow divided or cut off from some aspects of the individual's normal cognitive, motor, or sensory functions".

The renowned sceptic, The Amazing James Randi, conducted an experiment in which he blindfolded the operators in order to prove that any 'actual' messages were only the result of ideomotor effect or the subconscious. The results showed that not one understandable word was produced, nor any dates nor even a *"yes"* or *"no"*.

Ouija boards have been the source of inspiration for artists, used as guidance in writing or as a form of channelling literary works.

- Emily Grant Hutchings claimed that her novel **Jap Herron: A Novel Written from the Ouija Board** (1917) was dictated by Mark Twain's spirit through the use of a Ouija board after his death.

- Patience Worth was allegedly a spirit contacted by Pearl Lenore Curran (February 15, 1883 – December 4, 1937) for over 20 years. This symbiotic relationship produced several novels, and works of poetry and prose, which Pearl Curran claimed were delivered to her through channelling Worth's spirit during sessions with a Ouija board, and which works Curran then transcribed.

- In late 1963, Jane Roberts and her husband Robert Butts started experimenting with a Ouija board as part of Roberts' research for the book. According to Roberts and Butts, on December 2, 1963 they began to receive coherent messages from a male personality who eventually identified himself as Seth, culminating in a series of books dictated by 'Seth'.

- In 1982, James Merrill released an apocalyptic 560-page epic poem entitled **The Changing Light at Sandover,** which documented two decades of messages dictated from the Ouija board during séances.

- The writer, G.K. Chesterton used a Ouija board in his teenage years. Around 1893 he had gone through a crisis of scepticism and depression, and during this period Chesterton experimented with the Ouija board and grew fascinated with the occult.

- Early press releases stated that Vincent Furnier's stage and band name 'Alice Cooper' was agreed upon after a session with a Ouija board, during which it was revealed that Furnier was the reincarnation of a 17th-century witch with that name. Cooper later revealed that he just thought of the first name that came to his head while discussing a new band name with his band.

- Former Italian Prime Minister Romano Prodi claimed under oath that, in a séance held in 1978, the 'ghost' of Giorgio La Pira used a Ouija to spell the name of the street where Aldo Moro was being held by the Red Brigades.

- The Mars Volta wrote their album **Bedlam in Goliath** based on their alleged experiences with a Ouija board. At first the board provided a story which became the theme for the album. Strange events allegedly occurred during the recording of the album: the studio flooded, one of the album's engineers had a nervous breakdown, equipment began to malfunction, and Cedric Bixler-Zavala's foot was injured. Following these bad experiences the band allegedly buried the Ouija board.

- Aleister Crowley had great admiration for the use of the Ouija board and it played a passing role in his magical workings. Jane Wolfe, who lived with Crowley at his infamous Abbey of Thelema, also used the Ouija board, crediting some of her greatest spiritual communications to use of this implement. Crowley also discussed the Ouija board with another of his students, and the most ardent of them, Frater Achad (Charles Stansfeld Jones): it is frequently mentioned in their unpublished letters. In 1917 Achad experimented with the board as a means of summoning Angels, as opposed to Elementals. In one letter Crowley told Jones: *"Your Ouija board experiment is rather fun. You see how very satisfactory it is, but I believe things improve greatly with practice. I think you should keep to one angel, and make the magical preparations more elaborate."*

savage beauty
rediscovering the art and darkness of alexander mcqueen

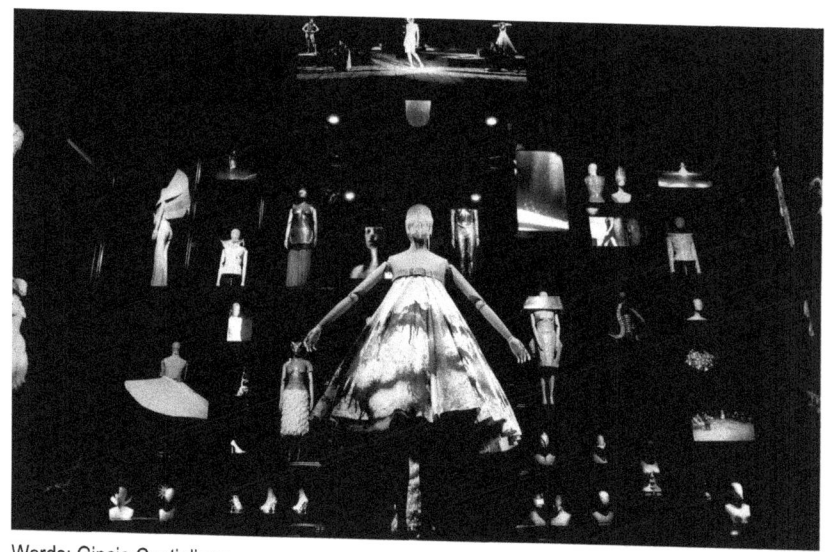

Words: Gipsie Castiglione

I find beauty in the grotesque, like most artists. I have to force people to look at things.'
Alexander McQueen

I don't recall which exact magazine I first encountered Alexander McQueen in, but something about his clothes, style, appealed straight away. In that mysterious way that one is instinctively drawn to music, artists, words, he spoke my language, silently, covertly, I guess some may say semiotics or something of that ilk.

There was something so fresh and new about his work, even if by then shock tactics and fetishism were already overused on the fashion world. Alexander McQueen expressed his influences, as varied as they were - be they the slow-slung jeans of the hip hop boys, the gothic morbid romanticism of Poe or the hardness of the gay leather fetish scene, the more salubrious the inspiration, it seemed all the more magnificent once translated by his masterful skill and glorious vision.

After years of admiring him, I finally acquired my first pieces. I was working in Harrods and was very friendly with the ladies in the international designer room. One morning I received a call from them saying *"McQueen has just arrived, we are putting the collection out tomorrow, there's only a few pieces, come up and take a look"*. I ran up the stairs two at a time! The collection was called *It's a Jungle Out There*, and I picked out a single breasted jacket and two pairs of trousers - my ass was pretty fabulous in my twenties but the skill of the McQueen cut made it look sublime!

More pieces came and went over time, but I still have those three. They will most probably never fit me again, but I will treasure them forever, like diary entries from my youth.

When I read about the Met's *Savage Beauty* exhibition in 2011, I longed to go to New York to see it, but unfortunately finances at the time put a resolute 'no' to that fancy. But then - after what seemed like an eternity - it was announced that the show would be coming to the V&A in London in 2015, and it made my year!

I knew it would be an unforgettable experience, and probably one to be repeated several times. The curation of the show and collaboration of the two greatest fashion museums in the World was always going to make that likely, but it would also be a personally emotional journey. I recall being saddened reading the news of his suicide, a day or two before his mothers funeral - it seemed such a tragic loss of an incredible talent while still so young and at the peak of his career. But it was seeing his work at the 2013 Isabella Blow exhibition in Somerset House that first moved me to tears (my boyfriend teases me about suffering from Stendahl syndrome - that being confronted with beauty renders me an emotional wreck). There was something heart breaking about the exhibition - the thought of these two pioneering talents, colleagues and friends, both taking their own lives was very poignant. So I was well prepared for the emotional experience that the V&A exhibition promised to be.

It did not disappoint.

The V&A managed to add an extra 60 or so pieces to the hugely successful Met show (viewed by over 650,000 people and one of the most successful exhibitions ever held there) so it was definitely worth waiting for the London homecoming show. Clearly, lots of people where in agreement because the show would become the most popular V&A exhibition of all time, even outstripping the highly publicised and more obviously populist David Bowie show a couple of years earlier.

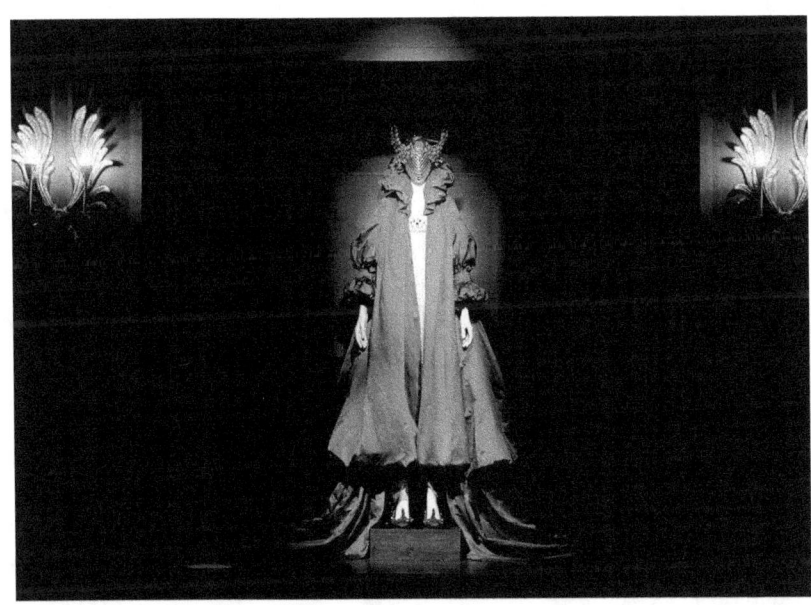

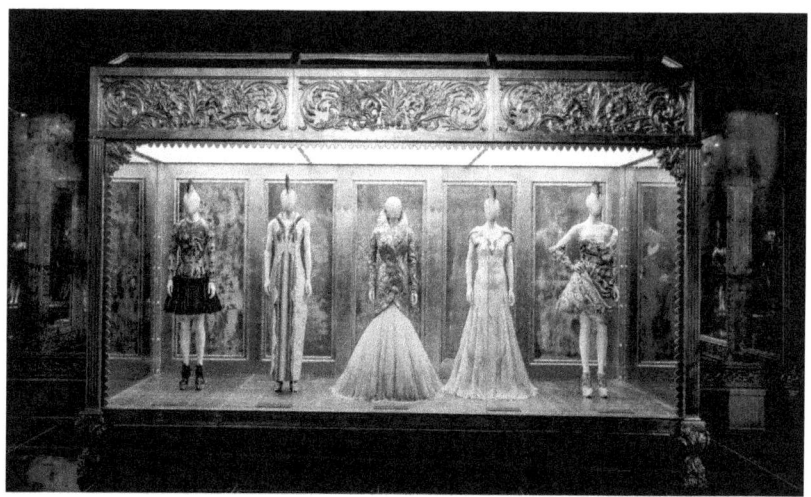

LONDON

Each thematically separated section of the McQueen exhibition was given a different name, though you might not have realised that at the time. The opening section was named after his home city and cultural passion. *"London is where I grew up. It's where my heart is and where I get my inspiration"*, said McQueen, the son of an East End taxi driver who left school at fifteen to become a tailor's apprentice on Savile Row, moving on to take an MA in fashion at Central St Martins.

The opening image was the artist himself, huge and holographic, a confrontational 'living' image of the dead designer's face morphing into a metallic skull - one of the motifs of death and morbidity that ran throughout his work - that lead us into the first room.

This section was very much an introduction to his work - a variety of his iconic styles like the infamous Bumsters that so shocked the fashion editors in the early 1990s, but were partly inspired by London street wear (and the notorious 'builder's bum') and played around with ideas of expanding the torso and fetishising the lower back. This section was an effective way of introducing the viewer who might not know McQueen's work - a trailer of sorts for what was to come.

Turning the corner was thrilling, giving the opportunity to see some of his graduation pieces, a collection called *Jack the Ripper Stalks His Victims* - famously purchased in its entirety for £5000 by Isabella Blow, who would recall hassling his mother on the phone endlessly until he agreed, and then taking him to cash points, paying £100 a week for pieces delivered in black bin bags. The tailoring skills picked up at Gieves and Hawkes (where he apparently would stitch 'I'm a cunt' into Prince Charles's suit interlining) were evident in these early pieces, suggesting early on the work of a master tailor who would go on to win the British Designer of the Year award four times and be voted International Designer of the Year 2003.

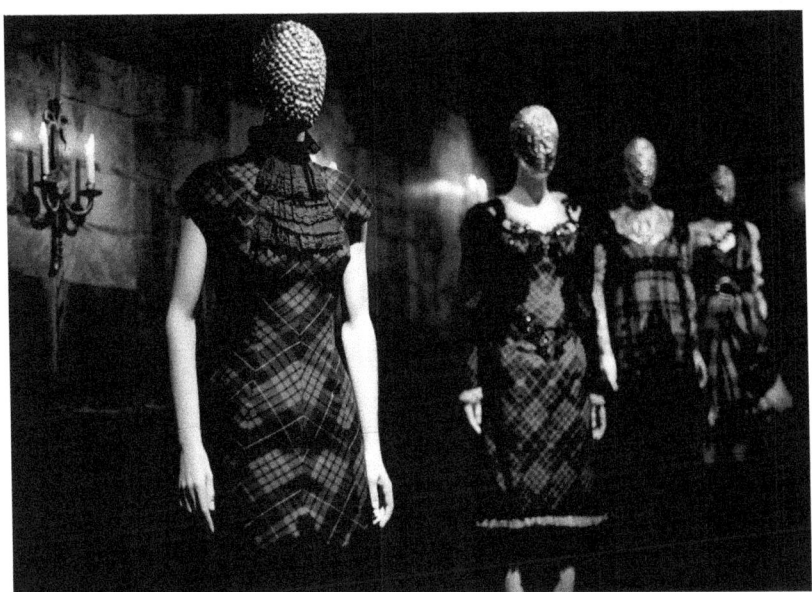

A GOTHIC MIND

'There has to be a sinister aspect, whether it's melancholy or sadomasochist. I think everyone has a deep sexuality, and sometimes it's good to use a little of it – and sometimes a lot of it – like a masquerade.'
- Alexander McQueen

The exhibition seemed threaded together with McQueen quotes - and to me, the above spoke the loudest, perhaps because of my personal interest in the gothic, the fetish silhouette that seemed to be inherent in me even as a child. This room was full of dark, melancholic and erotic fairy tale imagery, as inspired by the fetish club world as by any traditional fashion influences. Laden with black beaded mourning Victoriana and divine Mr Pearl corsets in the finest silk and lace, the threatening black leather masks that hooded the mannequins added a sense of foreboding to create a dreamlike Sadean masquerade that could never really exist. It was here where any sense of 'safety', of respectable mainstream fashionista tastes were challenged, as things became more unsettling and dark.

ROMANTIC PRIMITIVISM

The sense of challenging convention and modern sensibilities would continue, in a different way, in the next room. In a world where people fret about 'cultural appropriation', the idea of 'primitivism', the 'noble savage' and the 'uncivilised' man of the Amazon or Yoruba mythology living in harmony with nature becomes more confrontational now than in the late 1990s, when McQueen was creating his It's a Jungle Out There collection. Ethnographic imagery and the use of materials associated with African fashion play with a collective Western memory of conquest and colonialism, something that McQueen himself acknowledged: *"Fashion can be really racist, looking at the clothes of other cultures as costumes. That's mundane and it's old hat. Let's break down some barriers."* This gallery evoked the feel of H.G. Wells and **The Island of Dr Moreau**'s 'humanimals', and the idea of the fashion machine being predatory and the creatives - and consumers - being the prey. The genius could be found in the detail

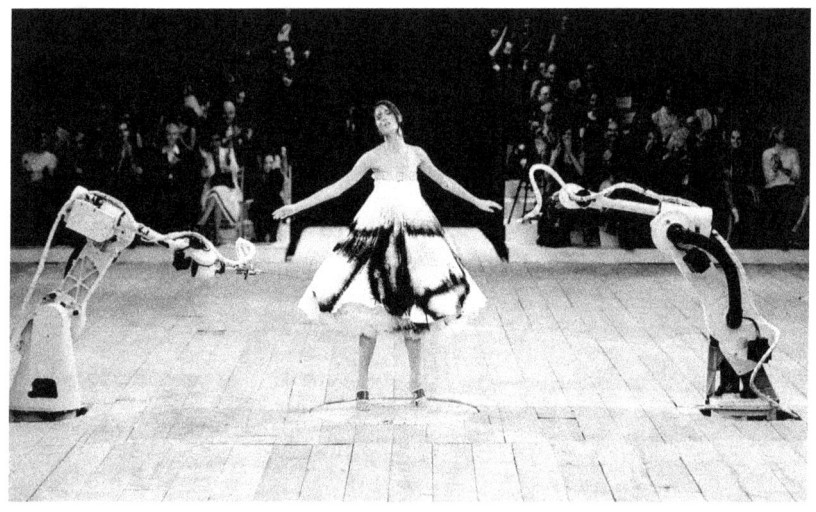

- sublime beading and minute detail that elevates the street inspiration into art, bringing an animalistic sexuality that was inherent in McQueen's persona.

ROMANTIC NATIONALISM

McQueen may have been a London boy, but as the name suggests, he had Scottish roots. *Highland Rape* in 1995 explored this, and his ideas of Scottish nationalism - and years later, his collection *The Widows of Culloden* took inspiration from that famous final stand of the Jacobite Risings (*"what the British did there was nothing short of genocide"*, he would comment). Walking through this room, with its perfect symmetry and lighting resembling a display room in a heritage museum, and the wood panelling giving a scent that felt very traditional and historic - very British, in fact, despite his misgivings. To keep the symmetry of tartan plaid while tailoring to the physique shows the absolute genius technique that he had. Overlaid with lace appliqué, broderie anglaise adding a glamorous femininity to such a traditionally heavy material, the strict colour codes of red, white and black added to the sense of formality, with undertones of playful fantasy. The mistress of ceremonies, holding court at the end of the room, brought a regal flourish that brings a romanticism and grandeur to the gallery.

CABINET OF CURIOSITIES

Nothing could have prepared me for the visual cacophony of this vast, seemingly endless, impossibly crammed yet perfectly collated series of imagery - video footage of catwalk shows and fashion event happenings mixed with full outfits, headpieces, shoes and accessories, creating a deliberate sensory overload that had the audience straining their heads to the ceiling and down to the floor in an effort to take everything in. A third larger than in New York, this was almost too much - if nothing else had this effect, then this room alone demanded a repeat visit just to be able to absorb all on offer. Sadly, as with any exhibition this popular, the sheer number of people and the limited time at hand made one rush through far more quickly than is comfortable, and in this room, that was especially notable. Luckily, being there towards closing time meant that there was at least enough room to pause and reflect on the detail and the glory.

This room represented many of the incredible collaborations that brought the McQueen shows to their theatrical heights, most notably with Shaun Leane, the London-based jeweller, who was a partner in crime until the end, and milliners Philip Treacy and Dai Reese, whose headwear would complete so many of the looks. The whole room seemed to orbit around the legendary white broderie anglaise dress in which a terrorised looking Shalom Harlow was assaulted by spray-painting robots in a 1999 performance that was part **Demon Seed**, part Survival Research Laboratories. I would defy anyone who had experienced this room to ever forget it, and if any point of the show was going to have that Stendahl Syndrome effect on me - or anyone - this was it.

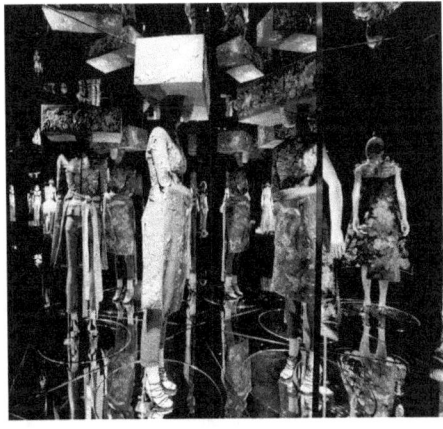

ROMANTIC EXOTICISM

Beyond the central mindfuck of the *Cabinet of Curiosities*, there was suddenly serenity and a certain return to the issues of cross-cultural influences, in order to further wind up those who have no sense of humour (or humanity) and believe that the races should never culturally mix. The most striking memory for me here was the reinterpretation of the kimono, which McQueen delighted us with time and time again, and the sheer indulgence of the orientalist imagery - particularly Japanese culture - that fascinated him (and fascinates me).

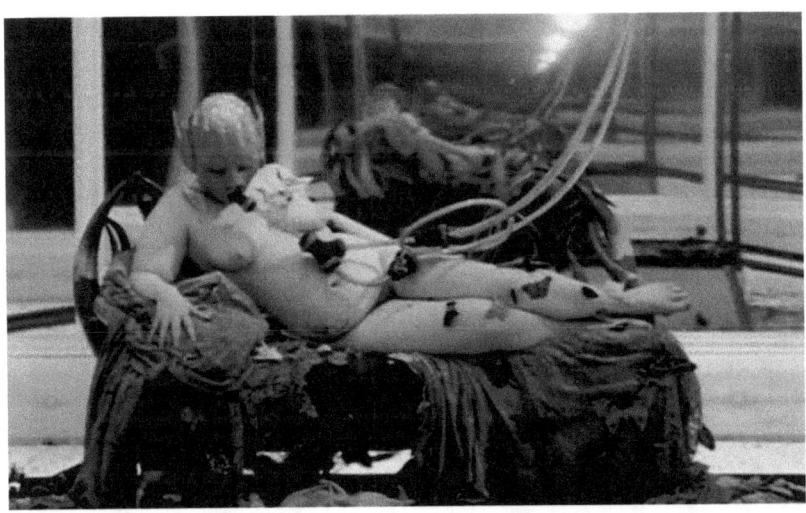

VOSS

Could this be the most memorable of all the McQueen shows? It's certainly the most talked-about. Joel-Peter Witkin, the famous American photographer who often dealt with the grotesque, the unsettling and the taboo - with 'models' ranging from sideshow freaks to dead bodies - was an influence on what was also known as the *Asylum* show, which challenged perceptions and ideas of what a fashion show might be, and confronted the egos and vanities of the glitterati gathered to view the spectacle. With a mirrored box that the crowd was forced to stare at for an hour before anything happened - the fashionista gaze turned back on itself - and then challenging ideas of catwalk beauty with the voluptuous and sexy **Skin Two** editor Michelle Olley - the antithesis of the anorexic and sexless catwalk model - attached to a breathing tube and a stuffed monkey, surrounded by moths, this was as much performance art as fashion show. Cleverly reconstructed for the exhibition, this allowed a hint of what the original impact might have been, with the glass-walled, padded cell containing mannequins wearing the most intricately beautiful pieces of the show, most unforgettably the red and black dress that starts off with shimmering sequins that become lush plumage. A massive video wall immortalised the Witkin **Sanitarium** photograph and McQueen's own version, and if the exhibition lacked the visceral sense of shock of the original show - short of hiring a live model to lie naked and tubed up all day, it's hard to see how it could be matched - it certainly recreated the visual aesthetics of that historic moment.

ROMANTIC NATURALISM

If there is a problem with exhibitions of this sort, it is this: you can sometimes be so overwhelmed by what has gone before, that the subsequent moments - the come-down, if you like - don't linger in the memory as much. It's helpful not to be thrown back onto the street (or into the souvenir shop) directly after the most intense moments; a sense of easing back into normality is helpful. But these are not the parts we tend to remember as well as those sensational rooms. The most striking moment here was the beautiful organza dress, which had both silk and fresh flowers giving that everlasting momento mori. This room was not, however, the final moment. It was a lulling point, giving us a false sense of safety and comedown, We were about to be plunged into a final point of sensory overload before we left.

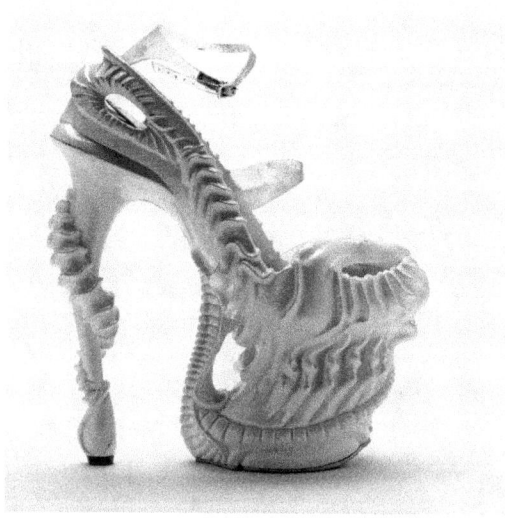

PLATO'S ATLANTIS

The final moments of the exhibition were perhaps the closest you could get to the experience of fighting for space at a McQueen show, as the crowd gathered around an astonishing, three dimensional projection of model Raquel Zimmerman floating and mutating into a sea creature, making it hard to see and harder to linger over. *Plato's Atlantis* was McQueen's final work, eighty per cent completed when he died. Undoubtedly the most accomplished of his work, it promised a new era that was never to be. The complexity of the digital printing of the

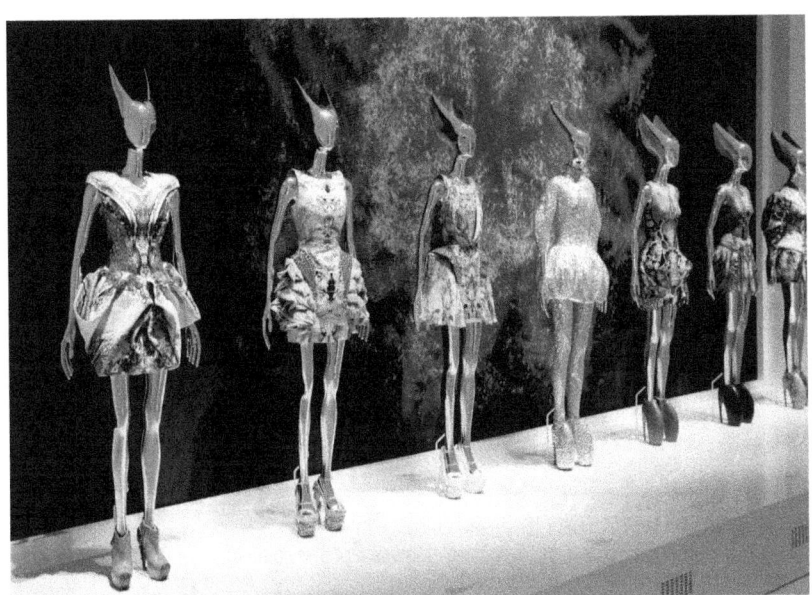

material, the intricacy of the patterns, the savour faire that screams from every piece - this was beyond anything that you could imagine, beyond anything happening in the fashion world. Based around the idea of aquatic devolution of humanity, the most enduring image of this collection (at least to a shoe fetishist) is possibly the 30 centimetre high Armadillo shoe, which totally reinvents our idea of the foot. A clear nod to Giger came with the **Alien** shoe, which captured the grotesque beauty of that artist's imagery. A heartbreaking finale that was a perfect contrast to the opening rooms of the exhibit.

I can only imagine what was yet to come, had McQueen not ended his life and his work so prematurely. While this exhibition is a complete record of his career, start to finish, I wish that it was instead incomplete, with more to come over the years. However, we at least have this extraordinary legacy for eternity - work that transcends mere ideas of fashion to become, unquestionably, high art. McQueen once said that *"I want to be the purveyor of a certain silhouette or a way of cutting, so that when I'm dead and gone people will know that the twenty-first century was started by Alexander McQueen."*

He can rest assured that he most certainly did.

not now, mr cooney

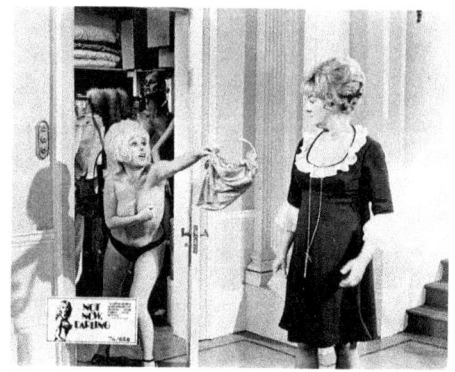

words: David Flint

It's hard to imagine a film more grounded in the time that it was made than the movie adaptation of Ray Cooney's famous stage farce **Not Now Darling**. In fact, should you ever want to send a **Guardian** columnist apoplectic with righteous outrage (admittedly, not a difficult task), then showing them this film should do the trick. After all, here is a movie about the womanising boss of an exclusive fur salon, who is happy to spend £4500 – and that's 1972 pounds – on a Mink coat for his would-be mistress just to get his leg over. Oh, and cast members Julie Ege and Barbara Windsor spend much of the film almost naked. Short of a comedy homosexual and some casual racism, it's hard to imagine how this could be more offensive to your modern socially aware viewer.

But **Reprobate** readers, being made of sterner stuff, should be able to accept this on face value, and while it's not exactly sophisticated humour, the film is fairly entertaining on its own level. Leslie Phillips – of course – plays the philandering Gilbert Bodley, keen to get into the knickers of sexpot Julie Ege – and who can blame him? Through a series of contrivances, he has to buy her a mink coat, but to avoid her husband (Derren Nesbitt) becoming suspicious, will sell it to him for the suspiciously cheap price of £500, covering the rest himself. Still with me? Things get increasingly complicated as Barbara Windsor turns up as the hubbie's mistress and is given the coat instead, Bodley's wife turns up unexpectedly, and Julie Ege's clothes are thrown out of the window onto the roof of a passing bus, leaving her literally in fur coat and no knickers.

Like all Cooney's farces, this replies on so many unlikely events and reactions that it becomes impossible to make much sense of what is going on, but the whole thing moves at such a furious pace that you hardly have time to think about how nonsensical it is. If you've seen similarly hysterical farces like **No Sex Please, We're British**, you'll recognise the frantic series of misunderstandings and the mockery of British sexual attitudes (I was genuinely surprised that a vicar didn't turn up at some point), and the cast of familiar faces are all old hands at this sort of thing – the exceptions being Ege, who doesn't have to do much apart from look sexy (which she does rather well) and writer Cooney, who has a major role as Bodley's long-suffering employee. He's unfortunately too prone to wild mugging to really match the rest of the cast. Director David Croft tries to expand the story, but the theatrical origins are all too obvious, with most of the action taking place in one location.

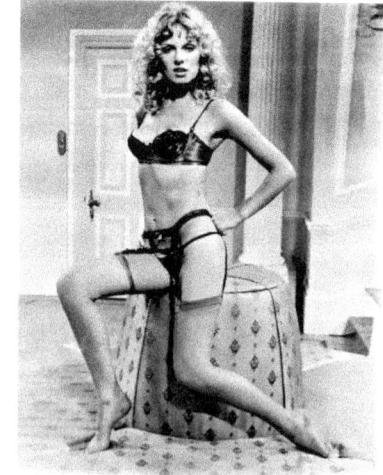

With some **Carry On** style flashes on nudity from Ege – brief enough not to challenge the PG rating – and some typical-of-the-time double entendres (Barbara Windsor offering to show people her tits – caged birds, obviously), this is very much in the British tradition of being both rude and innocent. Viewers may well marvel at the skill involved in having three cast members (including Trudi Van Doorn, aka Geraldine Gardner) almost naked for a large part of the film without actually showing anything, and it's fascinating to see how the themes of the British sex comedy could span, almost unchanged, from pseudo-family entertainment like this through to the X-rated antics of the **Confessions** films throughout the 1970s. There's something quite nice about that, and fans of the genre will find much to enjoy in this film.

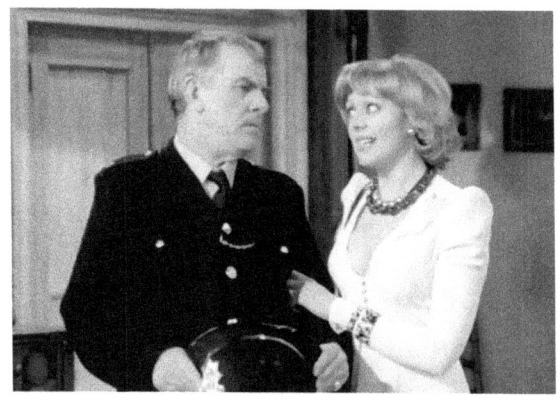

Not Now Darling clearly made enough money to justify a 1976 follow up – not exactly a sequel, but rather more of the same in the **Carry On** tradition. In fact, it seems that this was planned as part of a **Carry On** inspired series, which suggests a blinkered view of reality to rival that of Tyburn Films (who began making Hammer Films knock-offs a year after Hammer's business model had finally spluttered to a complete halt). By 1976, the **Carry On** films were effectively dead, with only the woeful and desperate **Carry On Emmannuelle** left to come. Trying to launch a series of family-friendly, naughty-but-nice low rent comedies at this time was hardly going to be a recipe for success in the era of the rather raunchier **Confessions** movies. To no-one's surprise, this was the last in the **Not Now** series.

The film is, once again, the brainchild of stage farce kingpin Cooney, who not only wrote it but co-directed and appears as one of the stars. It is based on his 1964 stage play **Chase me, Comrade**, and follows his traditional style of people running around from room to room trying to avoid bumping into others while coming out with increasingly outlandish excuses and ridiculous lies to deal with an awkward situation. In this case, it's a cold war comedy, with defecting Russian ballet dancer Rudi Petrovyan (Lewis Fiander), who accidentally climbs into the boot of the wrong car as his stripper girlfriend Barbara (Carol Hawkins) distracts his KGB minders with a 'topless' protest (in common with modern burlesque acts and in keeping with the requirements of the 'A' certificate, her nipples are covered with pasties). Rudi is driven off by the unsuspecting navel Commander Rimmington (Leslie Phillips), with Barbara and the Soviet minders in hot pursuit. Upon their arrival at Rimmington's home, all manner of nonsense begins, as Barbara and Rudi are helped by Rimmington's daughter Nancy (Michele Dotrice), her civil servant boyfriend Gerry (Ian Lavender) and put-upon gardener Hoskins (Roy Kinnear), who have to keep the presence of the defector from Rimmington, MI5 investigator Laver (Cooney) and a policeman (Windsor Davies) who turns up to investigate reports of *"a man behaving in an effeminate manner"* - Cooney apparently still thinking that such actions would be worthy of police investigation in 1976 – while trying to find a way for him to give the Russians the slip.

Naturally, all this involves people pretending to be other people, leading to – ahem – 'hilarious' misunderstandings about who is having it off with who, while Rudi behaves exactly like anyone on the run from the KGB would do, i.e. shouting loudly, mincing about and making no effort whatsoever to disguise who or where he is. Everything moves at a frantic pace, people running in and out of rooms and chasing each other through the garden continually before the film

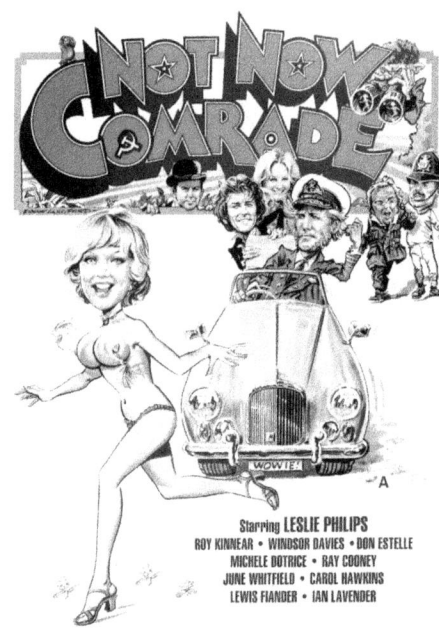

essentially runs out of steam and eventually fudges an ending that is remarkably indifferent.

Assigning any sense of logic to a farce is a pointless exercise of course, but within the universe created by the story, you do at least hope for some internal logic. **Not Now Comrade** unfortunately doesn't have this. While the increasingly ridiculous and complicated lies are a part of the grand tradition, you at least expect the characters to behave in a vaguely coherent manner within the context of the story. All too often here, people cause distractions simply by shouting, waving their arms around or stamping their feet like some sort of Tourettes sufferer. Compare it to the slickly produced madness of **Fawlty Towers** (which took the whole farce idea and perfected it in **The Health Inspector**) or even **No Sex Please, We're British** and **Not Now Comrade** feels strained and desperate. It also has too many characters, quite frankly – Don Estelle turns up as a neighbour towards the end for no reason other than because of his then-popular double act with Windsor Davies (he also sings the title song), while June Whitfield as Rimmington's wife is given very little to do.

Cooney's screenplay remains very theatrical – the early location shots and a few exteriors aside, it not only takes place within the one house, but mostly within a single room. There's no real effort made to open up the story or to give the audience a bit of a breather, which frankly is needed. The sheer frenetic nature of the film is honestly exhausting.

Because of that, it's hard to really judge performances. Phillips is suitably bewildered (and for once is not the lecherous middle aged man – when we first see him with Dotrice, I assumed she was supposed to be his wife, not daughter, as might have made more sense in a 1970s film) while Kinnear is excellent as ever as the long-suffering gardener, but everyone else has to be so cartoonish and hysterical that it's hard to tell if they are any good or not. Hawkins, who was bridging the gap between the **Carry On** and the **Confessions** films at the time, is cutely sexy, while Dotrice, who was sexy even when playing Frank Spencers long-suffering wife in **Some Mothers Do 'Ave 'Em**, is frumped up in a bad dress; Lavender plays a bumbling stick-in-the-mud quite well while Fiander makes his character so annoying that you really hope the KGB recapture him and work him over. Windsor Davies, meanwhile, plays another variation of his **It Ain't Half Hot Mum** character.

To it's credit, **Not Now Comrade** has the odd funny line and is pretty much painless to watch – the idea Sunday afternoon time waster, in fact (which is probably how many people first saw it, back when you could show films like this on daytime TV). The presence of so many well known faces from 1970s TV also gives the film a certain nostalgic charm for viewers of a certain age. But it does feel as though Cooney was running out of steam already – regardless of how many stage farces he would write in the future – and it's no surprise that the series ground to a halt with this film.

the lost classics of rock
don bradshaw leather - the distance between us

Words: Darius Drewe

So, just what *was* this spooky-looking bloke's name exactly? Don Bradshaw, Don Bradshaw-Leather, Don Bradshawleather? Was 'Leather' even part of his name, or the assumed monicker of the equally scary hippie chick adorning the back cover? For years, nobody knew: yet maybe precisely for such reasons, this near-impenetrable, impossibly hard to track down double album constituted one of the great lost grails of occult progressive rock. Even if you owned a copy, the unsolved mysteries continued to abound: never mind his bloody name already, just who was this clearly unhinged geezer, covered from head to toe in silver woad? More to the point, where was he now? And why had he seemingly never released anything else?

For yonks, rumours abounded that the culprit was none other than Enid mainman Robert John Godfrey under an alias: sure enough, the picture on the front did look a *bit* like Northampton's chief widdlemeister, yet whenever he was asked, RJG continually maintained he had nothing to do with the record, and, frankly, I believed him. For one thing, the chaotic, invocatory, near-Satanic sound displayed on all four tracks bore *no* resemblance to the disciplined, Royal College-trained classical oeuvre favoured by the East Midlands keyboard wizard - and for another, it simply didn't ring true that a gentleman of the openly gay persuasion such as our Bob would be even remotely interested in molesting a scantily clad female sidekick (as DBL is quite visibly depicted doing on the rear sleeve) Furthermore, whereas Godfrey, an ex-choirmaster, had always derived much of his influence from 'sacred' music, the elusive Bradshaw's massed collage of demented pianos, mellotrons, percussion and evil, intoning vocals seemed to come straight from Satan's bottom itself...

Then, suddenly, some ten years ago, the mystery was finally solved: according to his sister Geisha, who seemingly surfaced online one day out of nowhere, our arcane architect had been an Essex-born, classically-trained, reclusive Jewish chappie by the far plainer name of Don Bradshaw. Adding the 'Leather' suffix (like his other occasional name 'Odin') as a reflection of his newfound Pagan beliefs, he eventually relocated to West London where somehow, he managed to convince an unspecified major label (well, it was the early Seventies) to finance his 'magnum opus': upon hearing the result of his labours, however, said execs promptly had an attack of turtle touchcloth and withdrew the deal, leaving him no option but to form his own label and personally hawk his product round the numerous Camden, Portobello and Soho record emporiums where it would later be discovered lurking in bargain bins for as little as 10p. Suffice to say, the fact that it didn't sell even via this method also explains why he never cut another album - but over the years, its legend as a unique artefact of ritual/occult rock (even though it's barely 'rock' in any accepted sense) has grown and grown.

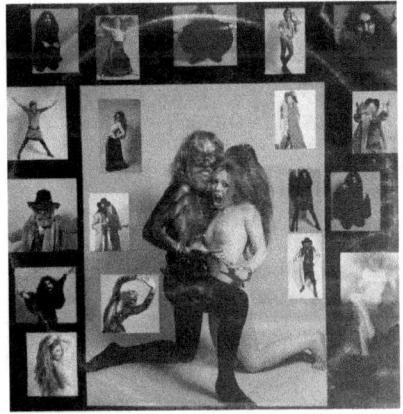

Sadly, Don himself- by all accounts, a troubled and solitary soul - died in the late Nineties, still probably entirely unaware of the high esteem in which his sole work was held by many: but at least the aforementioned sister seemed touched by her late sibling's cult status.

behind the door of the mitchell brothers

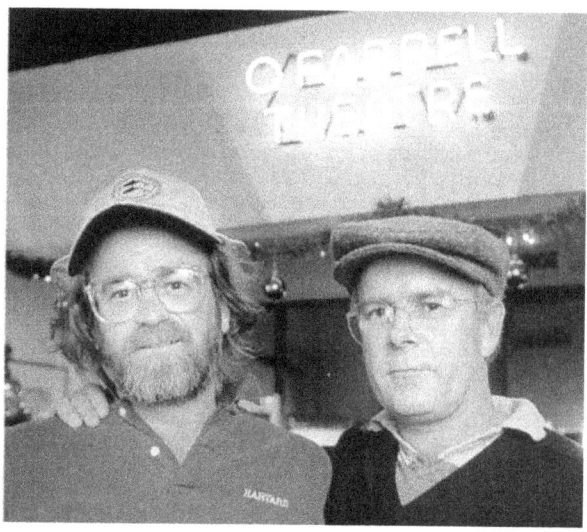

Words: David Flint

On February 27th 1991, police were called to a Corte Madera, Marin County home after reports of a shooting. Inside the house, they were led by occupant Julie Bajo to the bathroom, where they found the body of her boyfriend, porn producer Artie Mitchell. He's been shot three times - the final bullet had entered his brain through the eye, and killed him instantly. While officers were making this grisly discovery, their colleagues outside the house spotted a man acting suspiciously. As they approached, he was clearly struggling to remove something from his trouser leg. It turned out to be a .22 rifle, and a search of the man revealed that he was also carrying a .38 pistol. The apprehended gunman would turn out to be Jim Mitchell, Artie's older brother and business partner for over twenty years.

The death of Artie and arrest and subsequent trial of Jim would bring to an end one of American porn's greatest stories - a tale of hardcore revolution, rebelliousness and legal battling that helped shape the sex industry and created new stars. It all began back in the middle of the 1960s, when - as legend goes - the two Mitchell brothers caught an illicit screening of a cheap 8mm porn film. Sniffing the potential, the brothers decided to move into porn production themselves, but to do it better than anyone else. Jim took a course in film at San Francisco State University to get a handle on the technical aspects of movie making, and the two of them decided to fill their productions with better looking performers than were generally found in the stag films of the time. Investing time and money to secure interesting locations and buy decent film stock, the Mitchell's may not have been shooting great art, but they were making the effort.

They also benefited from the spirit of the age. In the second half of the 1960s, San Francisco became the love 'n' peace mecca, and the city would be flooded with open minded young hippie chicks. Suddenly, the kind of 'nice' girls who would previously have been aghast at the idea of even baring their breasts were cheerfully signing up to star in fuck films. A lot of them didn't even care about being paid.

The Mitchell's would soon open their own theatre, the O'Farrell, where they would show their increasingly ambitious films openly. The law fought back from time to time, but on the whole, turned a blind eye to what was happening in the small, unassuming building. Porn was still a secret - but things were about to change.

In 1972, when Gerard Damiano was shooting **Deep Throat** in New York, the Mitchell's decided to throw all their resources into an epic. Based on an anonymous porn novel, **Behind the Green Door** cost $60,000 to make. The lead role went to a young actress named Marilyn Briggs, who had previously stripped for the softcore Wes Craven / Sean Cunningham film **Together**. Changing her name to Marilyn Chambers, she cut a savvy deal with the brothers than gave her a sizeable fee and cut of the films profits. She also gave them the sort of publicity money couldn't buy: when **Behind the Green Door** went on release, it turned out that the actress seen taking cock in every orifice simultaneously was also the *"99 & 44/100% pure"* box model on Ivory Snow washing powder. The press went crazy, as did Proctor and Gamble

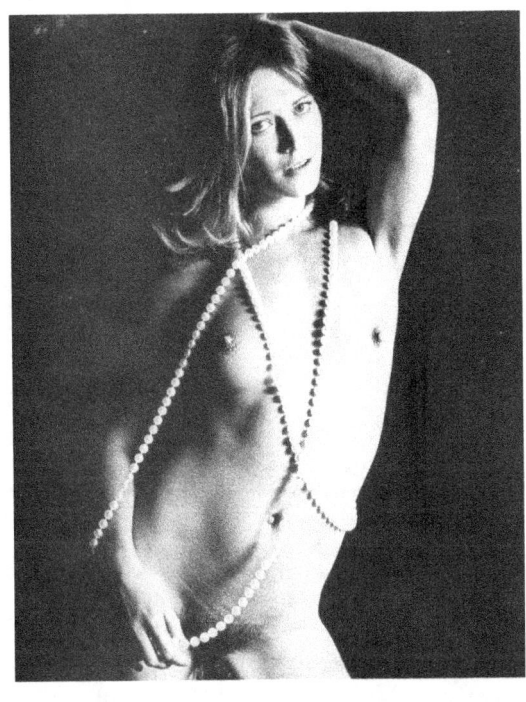

who moved to pull every box from their shelves... until they noticed sales had actually risen!

Behind the Green Door is a curious film - not especially explicit for the most part, it sits uncomfortably as a hybrid of porn, avant-garde cinema and empty minimalism - devoid of music or dialogue for the most part, and with almost static set-ups, the film is pretty hard work, especially if you are watching expecting an erotic experience. It ends with long, slow-motion solarised cum shots that are extraordinary to watch - this is not, by any stretch of the imagination, porn, even though that was both what it was made and sold as. Presumably, the audiences in 1972 would sit through anything for a few minutes of hardcore sex. And Marilyn Chambers is, it has to be said, a remarkable screen presence.

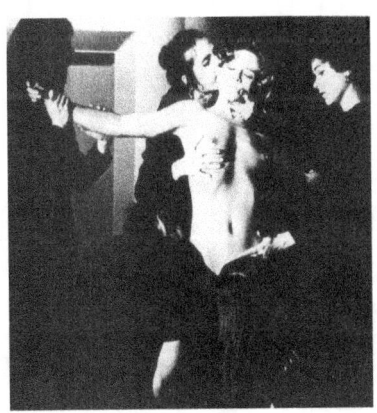

The film would eventually gross an estimated $60 million at the box office. Perhaps it made even more - the film was bootlegged by the Mob, who attempted to shake the Mitchells down - instead, the brothers fought back through the FBI, and it's their persistence in both establishing that porn films still qualified for copyright and in chasing violators that led to the FBI warnings that you now see at the start of all films released on home video in the USA. The brothers followed **Green Door** with a series of ever more ambitious movies - **The Resurrection of Eve** again starred Chambers, this time given some dialogue (her presence in **Green Door** is in body only), and is a much better - albeit more conventional - film. **Sodom and Gommorah**, on the other hand,

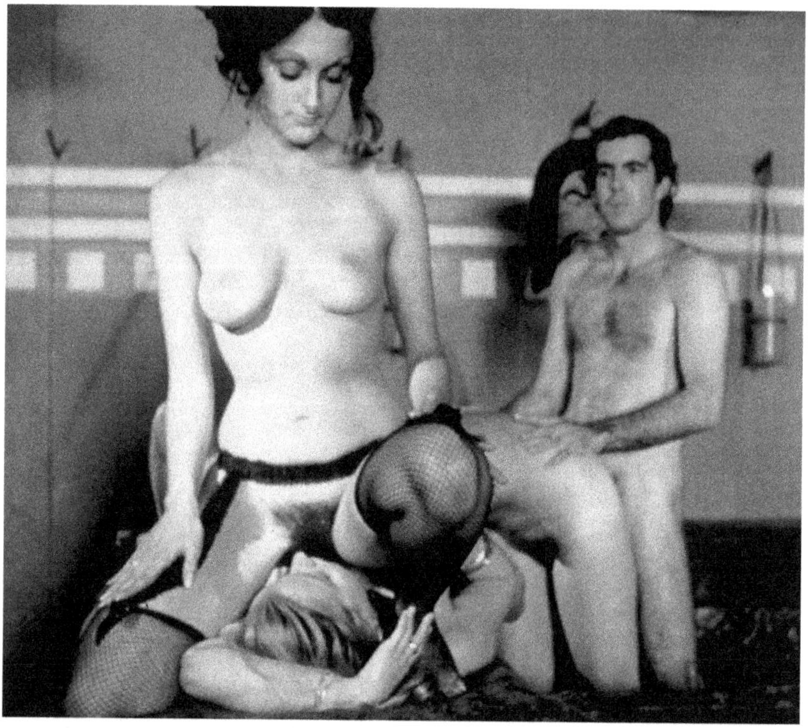

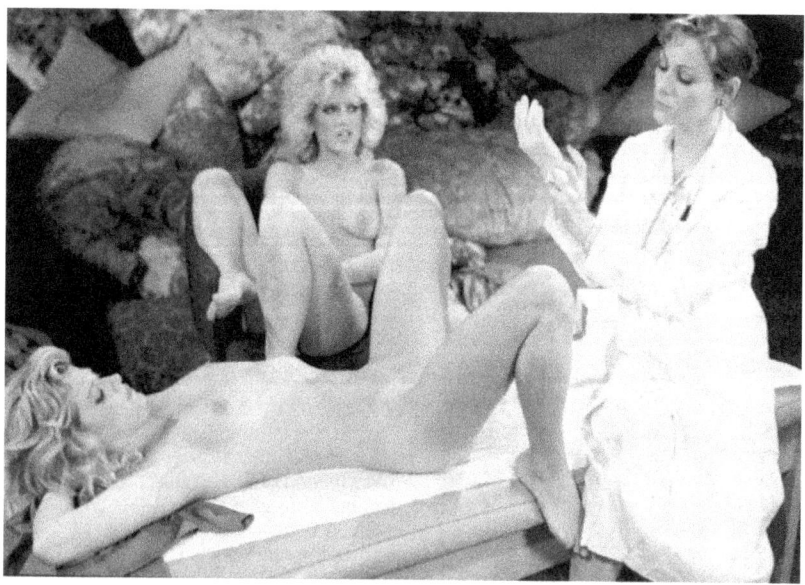

was a complete mess - a ridiculously ambitious biblical epic, costing millions to make (yet looking remarkably cheap and tacky) and suggesting that the Mitchell's were getting a little carried away, both with artistic ambition and cocaine consumption. Other titles such as pseudo-documentary **Inside Marilyn Chambers**, the BDSM film **Never a Tender Moment** and the star-studded **The Grafenberg Spot** (later pulled from sale when it turned out to be one of many films that star Traci Lords made while she was under eighteen) would be successful, but nothing ever matched the popularity of **Green Door**.

After a much-hyped but only mildly successful 'safe sex' retread of **Green Door** in 1986 and a couple of anonymous quickies the next year, the Mitchell's withdrew from film production, complaining that video piracy made it financially pointless (one can only imagine

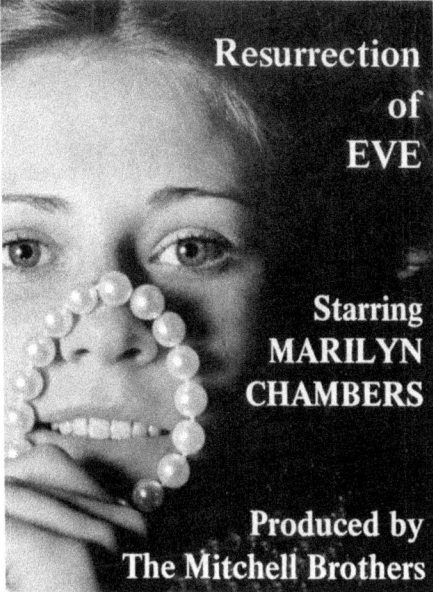

what they would have made of the internet and tube sites). Instead, they concentrated on the O'Farrell, where strippers and live sex shows were now the order of the day. They continued to have legal battles to fight, but always won. High priced lawyers, the liberal attitude of San Franciscans and the very fact that the brothers were surprisingly popular members of the local community meant that most cases against them were doomed to failure.

However, beneath the image of successful family men that the Mitchell's projected, trouble was brewing. Jim and Artie were very different characters. Jim had, by and large solid, developed from a party animal into serious, a sensible businessman. Artie on the other hand relished the image of pornographer and remained a substance-abusing maniac. He fucked the strippers and made an arse of himself in public, which in itself was fine - the Mitchells had a debauched reputation to maintain, and Artie was maintaining it. But he was spiralling out of control. Copious amounts of cocaine and alcohol were destroying his life and distressing those who knew him. One day he entered the O'Farrell when particularly wasted and fired a gun into the ceiling - an act which would see him banned from his own venue. Artie needed to be taught a lesson, and it fell to big brother Jim to deliver it.

We'll never know what really happened that night, but the general view - and the one Jim Mitchell relied on in court - is that Jim had gone over to Artie's in an effort to 'scare him straight' - maybe fire a gun into the ceiling to make him realise how dangerous his behaviour at the O'Farrell had been. The fatal bullet could have been a ricochet. The shooting could have been accidental, or just the result of years of frustration. One thing is known: less than a year before, Jim had risked his own life to save Artie from drowning. However, the killing caused a schism in the Mitchell clan, with Artie's children – perhaps not the most unbiased source – claiming that the killing was premeditated murder. But Jim was convicted of voluntary manslaughter and served just three years in prison, before coming out to continue running the family business. He eventually died of a heart attack in 2007.

violence and deceit

words: David McGillivray

If the world is ready for a cross between Derek Ford and Tommy Wiseau, someone is waiting in the wings. Here for the first time is a full critical appraisal of the astounding work of Steven Drew

Being a haven for megalomaniacs, cinema often attracts people who want to appear in films they intend to produce, direct and write even though they can't adequately perform any of these tasks. A notable example of how this unrealistic ambition can go horribly wrong is one Harold P. Warren, who made such a hash of the devil worship shocker **Manos: The Hands of Fate** (1966) that the film is currently Number 3 in IMDb's list of 'Bottom Rated Movies'. Probably I've forgotten even earlier examples.

Today, however, when the subject of quadruple-threat incompetence arises, there's no one to hold a candle to Tommy Wiseau, whose romantic melodrama **The Room** (made around 2001-2002?), set the bar to a new low. Several have tried to steal Wiseau's crown. One of my personal favourites is Richard Driscoll. Look him up. But Wiseau reigns supreme. This is remarkable because I saw the UK premiere of **The Room** at London's Prince Charles cinema as long ago as 2009. Today it's still playing the same cinema. It's still the **Citizen Kane** of bad movies. Surely it's time for a successor to **The Room**?

Step forward, Steven Drew.

By his own account, Drew is a former male model, who dabbled in the music business. He was in a failed group, Persuasion, which used Victoria Beckham for backing vocals. He then acted *"in UK theatre productions."* These are not specified, but in his Linkedin profile he mentions Questors, a well-known amateur dramatic society in west London. He has added himself to the cast of **Bonded by Blood** (2010), one of umpteen cheap films to exploit the Essex Boys murders in 1995. But he's not credited. Either he was an extra or his part was cut out.

He claims that **The Estate** (2011), his first film as producer/director/writer/star plus sundry other jobs under pseudonyms, *"attracted media attention."* I can't find any real evidence of this. The media attention may have consisted of two local radio interviews.

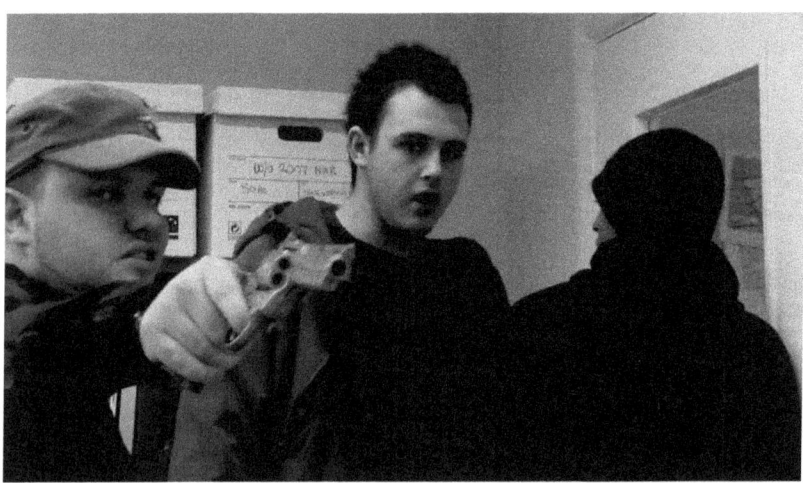

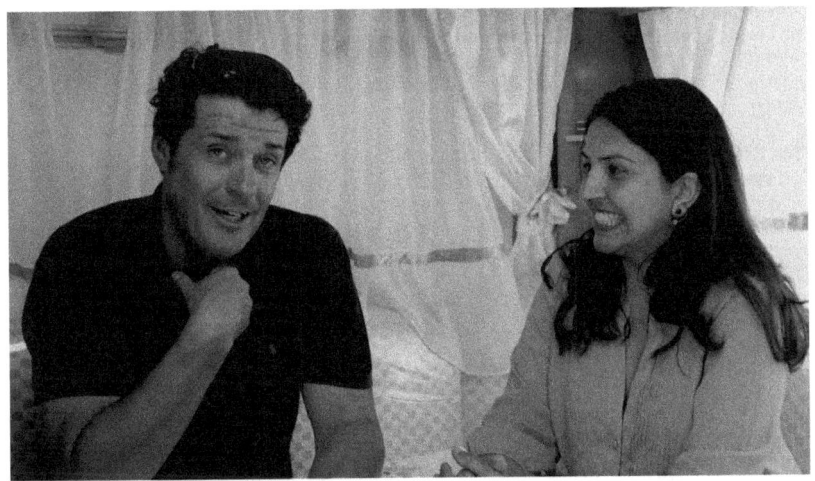

The Estate is a terrible old mess but not a distinctive one. It's a mere prelude to the magnum opus that was to come. Drew seems to think he's making shocking disclosures about life on a sink estate. But he's great at stating the obvious, e.g. Pakistanis work hard in their corner shops so they shouldn't be stabbed. Subplots pile up until it's impossible to know who's doing what to whom. The moronic dialogue just won't let up:

"You haven't got the fucking bollocks, boy"
"Who do you think you are? You're not my fucking dad"
"Yeah, I'm not going to be your fucking dad ever. I just want to fuck your mother"
"You fucking bastard. I tell you what, you shut your fucking mouth or I'll do you, I swear"
"Sure you fucking will. You couldn't cut a mince pie with that little fucking toy. Your father left you, you cunt…"
(Continues)

Brian Murphy from **George and Mildred** appears in a couple of scenes as an old gent in his living room and all I could think was - did Drew ever show him this script?

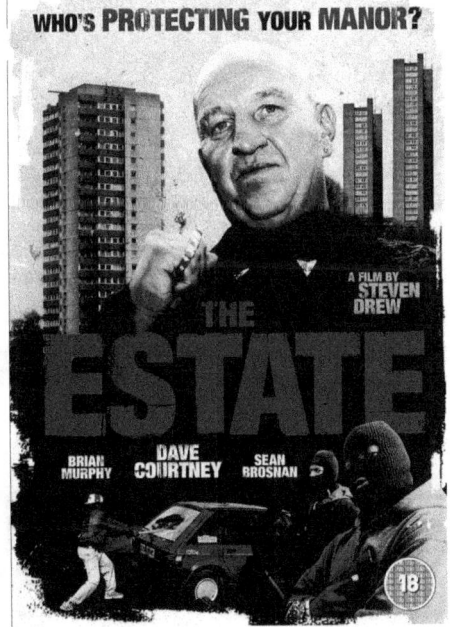

Other performances are pitiful. Drew plays a corrupt cop who's a throwback to swinging Soho. He thinks nothing of walking into a geezer's flat, stabbing him to death, and then calmly walking out, leaving his fingerprints on the door handle. The last vestige of credibility is lost when comedy gangster Dave Courtney turns up as crooked fight promoter, another plot strand that goes nowhere.

"The movie quickly established Drew as a serious independent film maker," says Drew. This isn't exactly borne out by the reviews on IMDb, which are headed *"Terrible, terrible, terrible"*, *"Worst British film for years"* and so forth. 'Dano_Scores' writes: *"I really struggled to work out how the actor who played the policeman got the role, as he was one of the worst, until I saw in the credits that he wrote and directed it..."*

The Estate did manage a DVD release on the Arrow label. But the reviews on Amazon were in the same 'Possibly the worst film I've ever watched' vein as IMDb. All apart from the customer who wrote, *"This is a classic movie. I think it's up there with anything by Terrence Malick or Steven Spielberg."* There is always the possibility he was having a laugh.

In 2010 Drew did a YouTube promotion for the film, appropriately enough in a back alley. There is so much traffic noise that what's said is almost inaudible. But seven out of the ten comments speak volumes about the alleged activities of Steven Drew 'or whatever his name is.' It would be inappropriate to quote them here.

Interviewed by a member of **The Estate** cast, Drew mentions an upcoming project about a widow who discovers that her late husband was a swinger. It had several titles before surfacing earlier this year on a local TV station, London Live, as **Deceitful Love**. It is Steven Drew's pièce de résistance, a sex drama of such literally jaw-dropping ineptitude (my mouth really did fall open more than once) that it is unique - or to be more correct there has been really nothing like it for the past fifty years.

I've written elsewhere that **Deceitful Love** is an absolute must for British sexploitation fans. Drew effortlessly turns the clock back to Derek Ford's **The Wife Swappers** (1970), generally acknowledged to be one of the worst British sex films - cheap, dull, uninspired, badly acted and suffocatingly moral. The message fifty years ago was that extra-marital sex leads to ruin. But there was a reason why this genre of film was called sexploitation. As producer/director Stanley Long so aptly observed in 1982 it was a case of 'Look at this, please, but it's terrible, isn't it?'

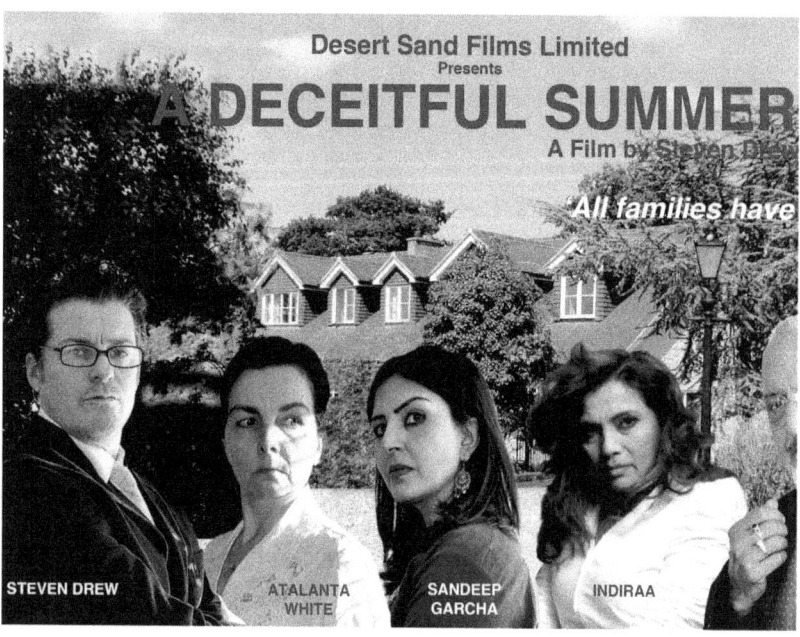

Drew is far too young to have seen **The Wife Swappers** first time round. He claims to have been *"born in West Lonodn [sic] 1967."* Like **The Room**, Drew's **Deceitful Love** is not a homage or a parody, it is an original, romantic melodrama done with enormous sincerity and an enormous lack of skill. Only one other British post-sexploitation film comes close to capturing a bygone era of cheap trash and that is Liam Galvin's **Killer Bitch** (2010). But Galvin, who's been around the block (sometimes with Dave Courtney) and can manufacture production value, is David Lean compared to Steven Drew.

Because **The Estate** may not have made a vast profit on its alleged £20,000 budget, Drew looks as though he had even less money to spend on **Deceitful Love**. I'd be surprised if it cost more than £5,000. The money is right up there on the screen. There are a handful of dull, suburban settings. The lighting is flat. This time round there was no chance of securing the likes of Brian Murphy. Featured roles are given to extras and bit players with predictable results. The performances of the blokes playing a solicitor and a doctor are indescribable.

But all this is nothing compared to the sheer barminess of Steven Drew's script and it's this alone- perfectly in keeping with the achievements of **The Wife Swappers** and **The Room** - that must make **Deceitful Love** a contender for the next **Citizen Kane** of bad movies.

The tawdry tale focusses on an Indian family. But the representation of Indian culture is about as authentic as **Curry and Chips**. After Sanjay (Satpal Lakhanpal) has succumbed not a moment too soon to a heart attack, his widow (Indiraa) discovers photo albums that provide convenient evidence of serial adultery. Indiraa does what only a soft porn suburban housewife would do: she joins a swingers' club. Not only that but she takes her mousey Brit neighbour Mary (Atalanta White) along with her. Within moments Indiraa has hooked up with the sleaziest old perv in film history (Gurdial Sira) and soon they're in a relationship.

Scenes in the swingers' club should by rights cause mayhem at midnight matinées. Expect audience members to wear Venetian masks and horses' heads and to join in the French farce-style dialogue (*"What are you doing here?"*). As in **The Wife Swappers** the sex scenes are awkward and perfunctory. Other scenes promise all the fun that fans have derived from **The Room**. As in the old days the wages of sin is death. Indiraa develops cancer. Her doctor's bedside manner is curt to say the least. Indiraa expires looking as though she's whited up. Finally Oliver (the indomitable Steven Drew) leaves a relative grieving at the graveside with a cursory *"Bye!"* Sorry if I've spoiled any surprises here.

Deceitful Love has a 2016 copyright date but another YouTube video reveals that filming began in 2013. Drew talks to Gurdial Sira, who speaks for us all when he says, *"At first I was a bit dubious about what was going on."* (Sira died shortly afterwards). As an interviewer Drew has his priorities: *"How do you feel about this script? It's a black comedy in some ways I guess…but it turns quite serious when, you know, we start acting out scenes regarding people having cancer and so on. How do you feel about this script?"* This time, perhaps significantly, comments are turned off.

Where the film has been for the past seven years is not clear although possibly in the meantime Drew managed to secure the services of Leee (**Body Talk**) John to contribute a handful of random songs to the soundtrack. Drew signs off his IMDb biog by stating that he *"currently has three movies scheduled for production 2018-2021."* With one year left to go, none has materialised. His Twitter account, which has six followers, hasn't been updated since 2011. But all this could change as more connoisseurs of grindhouse gems discover **Deceitful Love**. I can't be the only person who would pay good money to see whatever Steven Drew turns his hand to next.

jordan peterson vs gq
social science meets social justice

words: David Flint

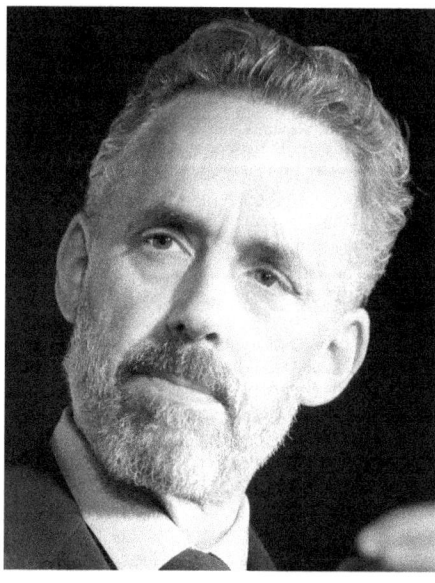

GQ is one of those odd magazines that has been around forever – thirty years, actually – and seemingly has a loyal readership, though quite who they are is anyone's guess – have you ever met a regular **GQ** reader? I certainly haven't. As a magazine, it seems almost as schizophrenic as **Vogue**. Like that magazine, this is a publication that has, for the longest time, been a bible of consumerist elitism, and yet now seems determined to pursue a social justice agenda while still pointing its readers at overpriced fripperies that they 'must have'. Champagne socialists, I suppose, and God knows, there are enough people out there who will spend more on a single lunch than some people make all month and yet still think of themselves as heroes of the downtrodden to ensure that this is not a case of cutting off your nose to spite your face. Currently, **GQ** is engaged in a hand-wringing, self-loathing *"dissection of masculinity"*, claiming *"rarely has there been a more confusing time to be a man"* while seemingly ignoring the reasons for the crisis – namely the constant demonisation of men that **GQ** and its right on like are involved in.

Recently, **GQ** sent journalist Helen Lewis to New York to interview Professor Jordan B. Peterson, author of **12 Rules for Life** and current scourge of the SJW set. Peterson built a huge following through his online lectures and his best-selling (2 million copies and counting) book, though Lewis – deputy editor of **The New Statesman** among other things – doesn't seem to have heard of him before his now legendary interview with Cathy Newman on **Channel 4 News**, where his straight answers and calm approach made her look like an idiot as she continually attempted to put words in his mouth. This, alongside his famous spat with the militant Trans community (refusing to follow a Canadian government mandate to use preferred pronouns for people or face the full penalty of the law) has had the rather unfortunate effect of making Peterson something of a darling for the Alt. Right and some of his supporters can be a bit ludicrous when it comes to naming video clips (I don't think Peterson really sets out to *"DESTROY FEMINISTS"* as some like to claim, and such claims don't help his cause one bit), though the idea that he is a Nazi – as his more delusional detractors imply – is pretty ludicrous. But Peterson is a man who has no time for the current sacred cows of the Left – he is a free speech advocate, dismisses ideas of a patriarchal tyranny and is, in the words of **GQ**, a *"heretic"* - an interesting phrase that perhaps inadvertently points to a truth that many of us have long suspected – that Political Correctness has become something of a religion amongst its followers, with any deviation from the Known Truths considered blasphemy.

More pertinent to **GQ**, Peterson has been seen as a defender of men – not in some swivel-eyed MRA way but by suggesting that (straight) men should not feel ashamed or apologetic simply for being male. That they have not, as individuals or a group, done anything that deserves the near constant abuse currently aimed at them, that they are not oppressors and tyrants, and that their achievements are every bit as significant as their failings. It seems a pretty reasonable idea, but in the febrile atmosphere of #metoo, the denial of collective guilt and the suggestion that men too can be victims (of violence, of false accusation, of societal pressures, of a lack of opportunity) is seem as an extremist and dangerous viewpoint by some.

I've read Peterson's book, and it's a fascinating, often dense but also insightful self-help book – as the title suggests, it is Peterson's own 'rules' for living a better, more productive life, which often goes off on strange tangents and makes constant reference to Biblical stories to finally make the point. Some of it is a touch esoteric, lots of it makes perfect sense, and it's hard not to think that anyone following these basic rules (*"pursue what is meaningful, not what is expedient"*, *"make friends with people who want the best for you"*, *"compare yourself to who you were yesterday, not to who someone else is today"* etc) would be a better and more productive person afterwards. It's hardly a right wing polemic, even if he does lay into Communism and suggest that life under Stalin was not the delightful egalitarian paradise that some will still claim. In fact, Peterson's philosophy often seems closer to Buddhism than anything. I would recommend reading it, and furthermore, I very much suggest checking out his live talks on YouTube, as well as his non-combative interviews with Joe Rogan. His interview with Helen Lewis is also worth a look, but despite her own analysis of the meeting as an equal battle of wits, it feels closer to the Newman debacle.

Why Lewis needed to fly out to the US to interview Peterson when he was doing a UK tour a month or so later is something that we may never know, but I'm sure it made her feel pretty important. And she certainly does seem to think of herself as *very* important, given that in her piece about the interview (**GQ** have certainly milked this 'confrontation' with their ideological enemy for all it is worth, with the video interview *and* an article by Lewis) she notes that Peterson hadn't Googled her beforehand – in other words, he didn't know who she was. But then, why should he? Presumably, Peterson has been interviewed a *lot* on his tour and hasn't delved into every interviewer's background. Perhaps he is simply confident enough in his own opinions not to have to know the history and beliefs of the person interrogating him (indeed, she notes that he asked her surname when being introduced, which rather suggests that to him, this was just an interview with 'someone from **GQ**' rather than a meeting with the jolly important deputy editor of a British political magazine).

Lewis' piece in **GQ** sets up the conversation as a battle of intellectual titans (though she carefully points out right at the start that her male friends are generally dismissive of Peterson – I imagine her male friends are pretty much all of a type, so that's hardly surprising). The entire thing is set up as a confrontation, which is perhaps not the best way to frame any discussion, but there you go – clickbait trumps facts every time.

There's frankly too much to go into here – the damn thing is 100 minutes long. But it's hard to see how anyone could look at this and see Lewis constantly landing body blows on her opponent. Certainly, she makes points where Peterson agrees and where he considers his answers – but then, one of the rules of his book is *"assume that the person you are listening to might know something you don't"*, and so only someone who goes into a discussion with a closed mind would be surprised that he might listen to your points). But Peterson's interviews are unusual. Most journalists are used to weasel words, obfuscation and defensiveness – they are trained to land blows on 'opponents' and put them on the back foot. That doesn't happen with Peterson. He considers his answers, won't be rushed and won't allow falsehoods – either misquoting him, or simply making statements that are opinion dressed as evidence – to go unchallenged. He tends to put the interviewer on the back foot and in the defensive role, and while it's a shame that socio-political interviews are like that, it's refreshing to see someone not being steamrollered by the media. Credit must, I guess, go to **GQ** and Lewis for allowing the whole video to be posted online, rather than printing a cherry-picked transcript (though Lewis' article is perhaps that).

In any case, Peterson seems to immediately get the cut of her jib and takes no prisoners – his points seem reasoned and concise, while Lewis pouts and, in the current fashion, posits her

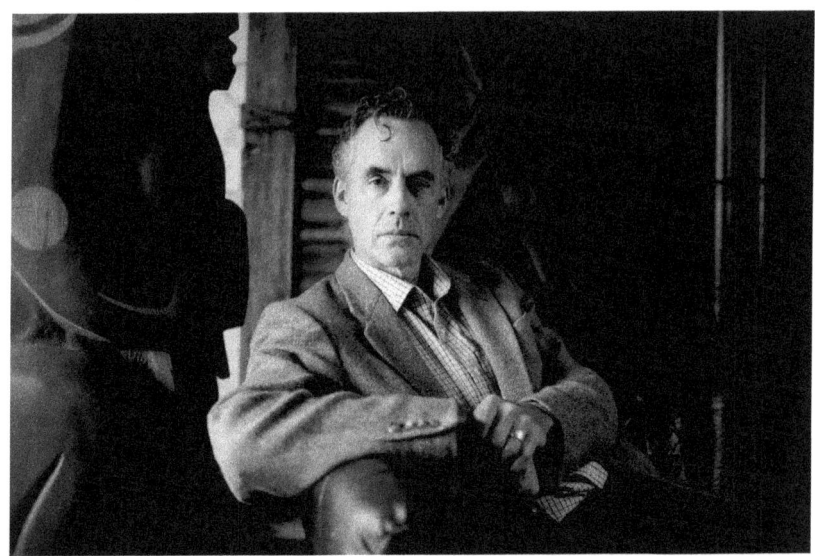

feelings as somehow equivalent – or superior – to facts. For instance, when the discussion moves to Count Dankula's infamous Nazi Pug video, and Peterson points out that people really *are* being prosecuted for telling jokes, Lewis responds that she did not consider it to be a joke. But of course, it was – it might not have been a witty joke, or an effective one, or a tasteful one. Dankula might well really hate Jews. But the video itself was still a joke, and no one should be comfortable with the idea courts (or deputy editors of **The New Statesman**, for that matter) should be deciding what qualifies as a legitimate joke and second guessing the beliefs of the person making it.

Let's look at one more example. Early in the interview, Lewis blusters and stumbles as Peterson questions why, given that she is the beneficiary of *"the patriarchal tyranny"* that she criticises, she doesn't surrender her job to someone more deserving – after all, if she believes in *"passing on"* her good life and how she is uncomfortable with people being filthy rich, surely giving that position to someone with just as much ability (we can all spout opinion, after all) but none of the social advantages. Inevitably, she blithely answers *"I don't want to"*, as if that settles the matter. But 'not wanting to' is surely the answer that all rich and powerful people have given for not making way for those beneath them. That's fine – no one should have to give up anything that they have worked for just because someone else has less. But then, they probably shouldn't talk about *"passing on"* the wealth and complaining about a *"tyranny"* that seems to have done quite nicely for her. Peterson points out that she is probably in the top one tenth of one percent of the richest people who have ever lived. *"I'm not sure I can help the Neanderthals"*, she smugly responds, but of course, Lewis is almost certainly filthy rich by the standards of most people even today, even in the UK – she's the deputy editor of the **New Statesman**, a writers for **GQ** who they will happily fly halfway across the world to do interviews, writes for **The Guardian**, has major publisher book deals and appears on TV with some regularity. I'll go out on a limb and imagine that her income and lifestyle are way beyond the reach of the average person in the UK, male or female. And as a graduate of St Peter's College, Cambridge (see, I Googled her!), she is surely much more a recipient of privilege than some working class man who has to get up each morning and empty other people's bins for a living.

But that's the uncomfortable truth that campaigners don't like to face – that real inequality in Britain particularly is still based on class, not gender. For people like Lewis to accept that would require admitting that they have, perhaps, achieved their place in life, their careers, their fabulous-but-socially-aware lives not through ability alone but also because of how well off their parents were – because they had opportunities that are still generally denied to working class kids in Rochdale, for example. For her to try to play the victim, and to suggest that she has somehow been oppressed by (quite literally) The Man, is the height of arrogance.

Why Jordan Peterson scares self-proclaimed liberals so much is easy to understand. He's no Steve Bannon. He's a conservative, but isn't some raging far right monster or deranged imbecile like Trump. He's an articulate, reasoned, polite and – in truth – socially liberal person who they really should have co-opted instead of seeing as a threat. Lewis' interview – and more specifically her written introduction to it - is another in a depressingly long line of pieces that seem determined to set Peterson up as some sort of Men's Rights bogeyman, when he's far from that. You don't have to agree with all his claims, all his rules and all his beliefs to see that the reaction to him by some on the left has been, frankly, hysterical. The demonisation of Peterson is, in fact, a classic example of just how fractured politics – and the politics of the personal – has now become. The whole 'with us or against us' mentality that doesn't allow for grey areas, for the admission of ever being wrong or for a reasoned discourse that accepts that no one side has a monopoly on truth and decency. The sooner we escape this regressive way of thinking and find a new way forward, the better.

EPILOGUE:

Since this piece was written, Peterson's life has spiralled rather spectacularly off the rails. He found himself addicted to benzodiazepine, after suffering anxiety and depression after his wife was diagnosed with terminal cancer. The highly addictive drug, and his personal situation, took quite a toll on his life, leading to sucidal thoughts and a mental breakdown that was captured in at least one interview. I can only imagine what Peterson was going through at this point, and it's not hard to feel sympathy for him as his life fell apart.

Unless you are a social justice activist, of course, in which case you'll take enormous pleasure at his decline. When news of his breakdown reached Twitter, the platform was abuzz with people - the sort of people who believe themselves to be good, decent sorts who are against hate speech - celebrating and wishing him ill. Often they would do so by saying things along the lines of 'I wouldn't wish ill on anyone, but...', the 'but' being the opening to wishing ill on anyone who doesn't subscribe to your philosophy. Along the way, Peterson was misrepresented as a macho guru, a fraud and someone who teaches hate - none of which is remotely true. It's possible to disagree with Peterson - and indeed, some of his beliefs are very much the opposite of mine - while still admiring his work, and understanding that his writing is designed to help people who are feeling lost in the modern world. That so many of those people are young men, understandably confused by their almost constant monstering in the media and academia, is something that GQ and its *"dissection of masculinity"* ought to understand only too well. But probably doesn't.

Peterson will hopefully come through his ordeal, and be back to cross swords with pinheads and the smug and privileged who like to wallow in their own imagined victimhood once again. In these confusing times, we need his clear-headed thinking more than ever, and if we disagree with him, we should do so with the same calm decency and politeness that he treats his detractors.

loverboys, dancing bears and partying hardcore
male strippers and horny housewives on the internet

Words: David Flint

If you explore the worlds of online porn – and let's be honest about this, you do – then you will be aware of the way that niche genres, once confined to one or two video releases, have now burst into the relative mainstream. I'm not talking about those featuring illegal activity here, but rather the curious fetishes and peccadilloes that might have once been considered too specialised for commercial porn producers to bother with but which now are out there en masse for the curious to explore.

I was first introduced to the phenomenon of CFNM – that's Clothed Female, Naked Male - by a porn star acquaintance who had appeared in a few of the films by made companies like CFNM Wave, where fully clothed women like herself (and it seems as though the makers of these films used a core collective of performers, the same faces popping up time after time) would tease and humiliate naked men.

These websites and the films therein were an intriguing variation on a BDSM theme, and as I explored the genre further, I discovered even more specialised variants. There was, I found, a whole sub-set featuring men with tiny cocks being laughed at by women. Well, that made sense for submissives, I guess. And then there were the male strippers, which seemed to be entirely aimed at the other end of the market, despite the fact that most heterosexual men would probably not be attracted to websites that advertised themselves as male strip shows. However, the emphasis here was not so much on the naked male undressing seductively – as in, say, a Dreamboys or a London Knights video of old that were made entirely for the same female audience that attended their live shows – as in their sexual interaction with the women in the audience.

Rather, the appeal was clearly in watching attractive women tossing off and blowing the strippers – that combination of the explicit and the forbidden, with the latter made clear by video clip titles that emphasised the fact that these were wives and girlfriends, morally loosened by booze and hen-night excitement. The footage claimed to offer an insight into what *really* happened at such events, and so pitched itself at both the straight male porn viewer who wanted to believe that he too could be a male stripper and enjoy this bounty of free sex, and the cuckold fetishist who fantasised about watching his other half cheating on him with someone hunkier, better looking, more endowed and more sexually capable than he might be.

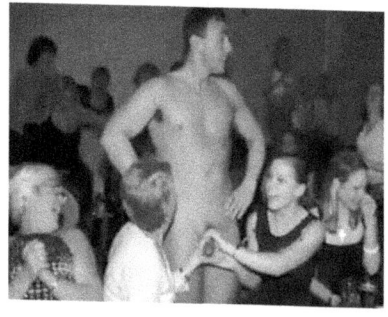

A scan of these type of films on assorted tube sites quickly reveals three market leaders. From the Czech Republic comes **Party Hardcore**, which would seem to have evolved from featuring private hen parties to a more consistent style, where a nightclub full of women enjoy traditional make strip shows while also enjoying sexual encounters with both the strippers and the male waiters, who would be quickly stripped of their clothing. Supposedly taking place in a real club in Prague, it becomes pretty obvious, no matter how much you might try to suspend your disbelief, that the sexual encounters here are almost entirely staged – the women who engage in full sex are clearly paid porn stars. But the fact that there are *so many* women in the club – hundreds – does suggest a certain blurring of reality and fiction, unless we are to believe that the producers actually hired all these women, including the ones who don't engage in any sexual activity or lose any clothing. And that seems a bit extravagant, budget-wise.

Similar in style is the American **Dancing Bear** site, which supposedly features footage of make strippers at bachelorette parties, but which is, again, entirely staged. These clips strive for authenticity, but the filmmakers can't resist over-egging the pudding. So a blow job will go on for ages, and brides-to-be will be screwed in front of their friends, and women take cum shots to the face, and everything just feels too much like a real porn film. It simply doesn't work as reality porn because even by Gonzo standards, it all feels *too* staged. Again, the large cast includes a lot of women who don't do anything, which makes you wonder how they are casting this stuff, but unlike the **Party Hardcore** films, there doesn't even feel as though there is the *possibility* that any of this could be real, even the clips shot on domestic cameras with wobbly, handheld style.

More interesting that both of the above is the British **Loverboys** series, which seems to be almost entirely authentic - there's the suggestion of the odd ringer in the crowd to get things going, but otherwise it feels weirdly real. The hen night crowds, the venues, the sheer British, domestic grottiness of much of it is the sort of thing that is too hard to fake convincingly, and the sexual interaction between the strippers – who range from cheeky chappies with hard-ons to chubby blokes to guys who are clearly coked off their nut - and the women is convincingly awkward and embarrassed.

Shot in working men's clubs and the like (one clip has a 'Northampton Rugby Club' sign at the back of the stage), this has strippers who are not especially hunky performing to/with an audience of all ages, sizes and levels of attractiveness. All of the clips online seem to have been shot in the early 2000s, before the new wave of morality swept the nation, and so it's not hard to imagine that the women who attended these shows, full of booze, bravado and female bonding, really *were* willing to pop a dick in their mouth or fondle a flagging erection, even with a camera pointing at them. Perhaps it's not so hard to imagine that similar things might be happening even now – I somehow doubt that #*metoo* and the new wave of sexual prudishness has really had much impact with the sort of women who go to hen nights at Northampton Rugby Club.

What's notable are the varied reactions of the women in attendance, from the very embarrassed to the shamelessly naughty to those - a distinct minority, it must be said - who seem genuinely turned on by the whole thing. The misbehaviour on display in these clip doesn't often seem to be driven by desire as much as it is wild liberation - women behaving in ways that society disapproves of and which we are told, even now, is not what good girls do - in the (dare I say it) safe space of the hen night, women really can let loose in ways that they might not be able to do elsewhere. The result is a joyful celebration of sexual freedom that contrasts wildly with the male audiences at female strip shows, where there is often the stench of guilt, shame and embarrassment. Certainly, you don't find men whooping, cheering and giggling while naked women parade in front of them. A shame really - what strip clubs need is a bit of audience appreciation, frankly.

The joy of a **Loverboys** clip, in truth, is not the sexual explicitness – because quite frankly, you can find raunchier stuff almost anywhere on Pornhub – but the sense of authenticity. That this is real life, real bad behaviour. . It feels like it is shattering taboos, not just sexually but socially too, and I'm all for that. And despite the best efforts of the new moralisers, I rather imagine – and very much hope - that it will remain forever England.

cancelling candy
how lou reed's celebration of diversity has been reinterpreted as a hate anthem

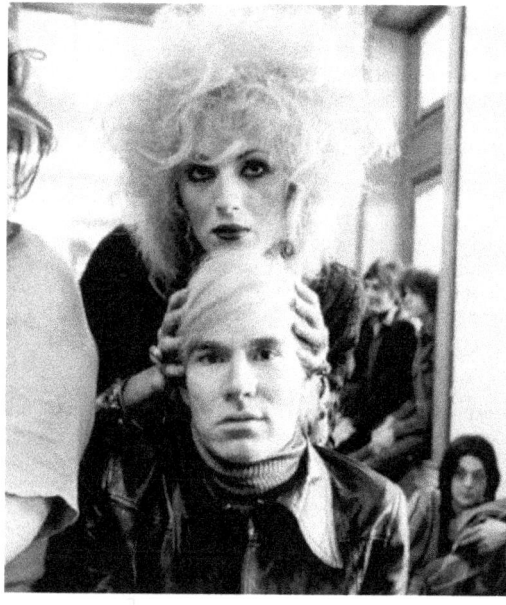

Words: David Flint

In our current world of offence culture, intersectional rivalry for who is the biggest victim and middle class virtue signalling (and I'm sorry, but if there is a better phrase to describe the following story, I can't think of it), there seems to be a continual competition to see who can come up with the most lunatic collision of all three of these social justice strands. The Guelph Central Student Association, of the previously obscure University of Guelph in Ontario, Canada, might not be the worst example of this, but their Facebook apology - subsequently deleted but of course captured for posterity by astonished readers - somehow seems to be an almost perfect example of pious self-righteousness, hand-wringing distress at possibly punching down, and an almost impossible to fathom level of cultural ignorance.

Their 'crime' was to play Lou Reed's **Walk on the Wild Side** during a campus event in 2017. Now, you might imagine that the 47 year old song has what we now have to refer to as 'problematic' lyrics for our easily offended youth. The reference to 'coloured girls' is always going to cause problems in some circles - these days, anyone covering the song might have to instead say that *"the girls of colour go"*, until the point that someone decides that that *too* is an offensive term. We can understand that, even if we will constantly point out that the context of time and history is important. Astonishingly though, that isn't the part of the song that was deemed upsetting. In fact, it seems to have slipped by unnoticed; either that, or intersectional outrage can only focus on one form of oppression at a time.

In fact, the thing that has caused the song to be cancelled - at least in the Guelph University region - is its transphobic lyrics. I assume, like me, you are both immediately aware of which lyrics that are and slapping your head at the sheer stupidity of the whole thing right now. But for those who might be in doubt, or perhaps somehow unfamiliar with the song, it's the bit where Reed sings *"Holly came from Miami, FLA/Hitchhiked her way across the USA/Plucked her eyebrows on the way/Shaved her legs and then he was a she/She says, 'Hey babe, take a walk on the wild side'."*

The Guelphers commented that *"We now know the lyrics to this song are hurtful to our friends in the trans community and we'd like to unreservedly apologise for this error in judgement"*, adding that the lyrics *"dehumanise and fetish"* trans people by suggesting that they are *"wild or unusual or unnatural"*. Well. Perhaps acknowledging some awareness of what the song is actually about, the statement continued *"While we acknowledge that the song was written with certain purpose and intention, we would also emphasise that media is not always consumed in the ways that it was intended"*.

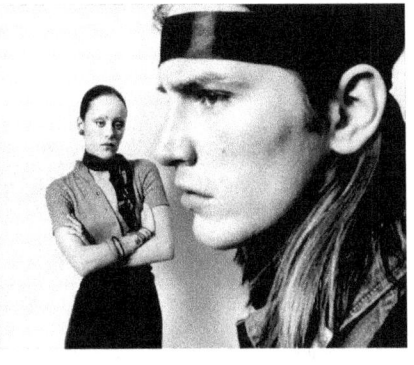

Certainly, this piece of media has not been consumed by the Student Association in the way that it was intended. **Walk on the Wild Side** is, of course, a biographical snapshot and celebration of the people Reed knew from Andy Warhol's factory entourage, including transgender superstar Holly Woodlawn (and fellow trans performer Candy Darling, also featured in the song but without direct reference to her gender status). The Factory was, of course, a famous gathering spot for the outcasts, the alienated and the socially marginalised, back when that sort of marginalisation meant facing problems rather more pressing than someone addressing you by the wrong pronouns on Twitter.

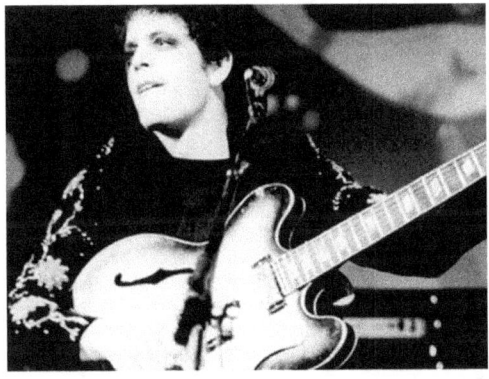

In 1972, these were heroic, daring and revolutionary people, and Reed had recorded a positive, supportive and revolutionary song as tribute to them, one that slipped transgenderism and what we might now call gender fluidity, gay sex, drug abuse and male prostitution past the radio censors and into the mainstream of culture, back when such things were still at the very fringes of society and seen as perverted and unspeakable. It was a rallying call to all outsiders, freaks and misfits. Subversive stuff that is now being vilified and silenced because of an imagined offence - do we need to even point out that apparently, no trans person had actually complained? - and privileged paranoia from people who have probably never had a wild experience in their miserable, painfully socially conformist lives.

Woodlawn, Darling, Little Joe Dallasandro and even Reed himself really *were* on the Wild Side, and proud of it. Taking that away from them is to deny their reality and the very real battles they went through at a time when they were genuine outsiders. Smugly dismissing that struggle because it somehow upsets your delicate sensibilities is disgraceful, and pushing them back into the margins of society is nothing short of despicable. Shut up and check your own fucking privilege, you hand-wringing spoiled brats.

memoirs of a reprobate

Words: Leslie Hopewell-Ash

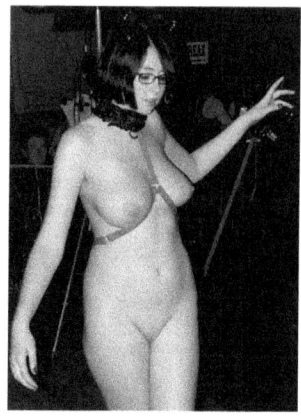

I was always fascinated by the idea of an SM club. When I was a fourteen year old girl my older sister, who had recently moved to London, told me about the Batcave and early warehouse parties like the Dirtbox, and about a secret rubber-leather club that went on, called Skin (sic). She hadn't been to it herself, but she knew somebody who knew somebody who had, and she said people led each other around on dog leads and got whipped on the dancefloor. An intense desire sprang up inside me to go there but my desire was so secret and furtive that I denied it, and told my sister *"it sounds disgusting. Surely you don't want to go somewhere like that..."*. She was crestfallen, and never did go.

It was 1987 before I finally went to Skin Two (as I discovered it was really called). I had been living in London for four years, and felt myself to be at something of a loose end socially. Kinky sex seemed to have a high profile that year. **Blue Velvet** came out, with Isabella Rossellini's husky pleas to be hurt, and Grace Lau's exhibition of black-and-white photography, at the Submarine Gallery in King's Cross, got a lot of publicity that summer.

It was at the Submarine Gallery that I bought my first copy of **Skin Two**. I was desperately excited and couldn't wait to get home and read it; I was too embarrassed to read it on the tube. When I got in I hid from my flatmates in my bedroom and read it from cover to cover, ignoring all else. It seemed like a window into a bizarre fantasy world, peopled by exotic, rubber-clad ectomorphs, and I longed to enter it. When I was a little girl I had always fantasised about being a member of a secret society, but had never found one that was appropriate. This seemed perfect and compelling, an underground world of sophisticated, kinky elites.

London listings magazine **City Limits** (now sadly defunct) was full of adverts that summer from perverts wanting to meet other perverts (I think they must have had a more libertarian advertising policy than their rival **Time Out**). I placed one too. Although in the column called Heartlands I was not seeking a partner but simply contacts to experience this strange clubbing world with.

I was astonished by the hundreds of replies I received, and they kept on coming. I dined out free for weeks with a variety of charming and attractive men, all of whom were seeking a kinky girlfriend. Although I had not been seeking a partner (I'd recently ended a long-term relationship) the sheer force of interest was overwhelming and I eventually succumbed to the attentions of a rather suave, sinister character whom I shall call George. We attended many fetish clubs and parties together and I quickly became known as his sex slave.

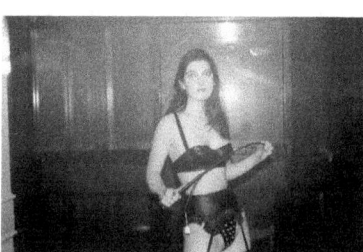

The first kinky club I attended was the imaginatively titled Fetish Fetish at Turnmills on a Saturday night in the Summer of 1987 (this was long before the days of Trade, at the same venue). I remember what I was wearing: a black leather mini-skirt from Kensington Market that cost £30, a black cotton top, sheer black stockings from the hosiery department of John Lewis, and black patent high-heeled shoes from Dolcis.

It was a slight disappointment from what I'd imagined: the people were weirder, uglier, smaller, not as beautifully dressed as the types in **Skin Two**. It was not very well attended, and everybody seemed to know each other, though this was probably just my feeling of insecurity as a newcomer. George brought along a dog-collar and lead in a plastic bag, for me to wear (Many people seemed to bring along little plastic bags of mysterious, kinky apparatus, which they clutched awkwardly and furtively). Towards the end of the evening I let George put the dog collar around my neck, with some reluctance but with a belief that I was somehow experiencing the whole thing. Some noisy spanking went on. We sat on the balcony, looking down on the people below. Nearby on the balcony, in the darkness, a man was giving a transvestite a blowjob. They kept glancing slyly over at me, probably to see if I was watching. The DJ was playing **It's A Sin** by the Pet Shop Boys, which was a chart hit that summer. Whenever now I hear **It's A Sin** by the Pet Shop Boys I think of Fetish Fetish at Turnmils and that man giving the transvestite a blowjob.

George was an eccentric person, a wealthy *bon viveur* with time on his hands and no apparant source of income. I believed him to be a millionaire who had made his fortune very young. He spent money on me, taking me abroad, and we sampled the SM scene in Holland, which I found to be nastier and more commercial than in England. Some of his fantasies, however, were a bit strong and he was soon bullying me to perform in my sex slave role for his friends, both male and female, at parties. The relationship quickly palled when I got fed up with being spanked all the time, and when I found out he was actually an old age pensioner, young-looking for his age, which accounted for his general caginess about things and his startling knowledge of life in the Second World War. I gave him the elbow and started to explore my dominant side.

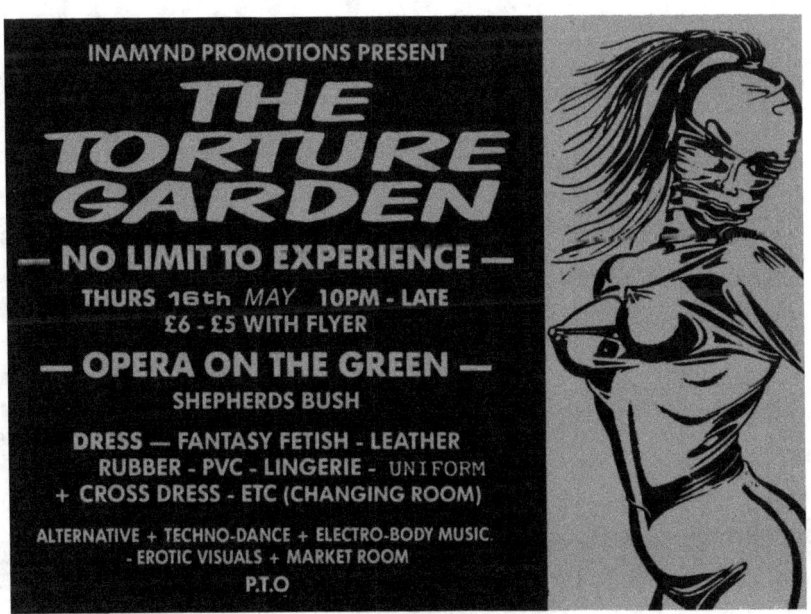

the Reprobate

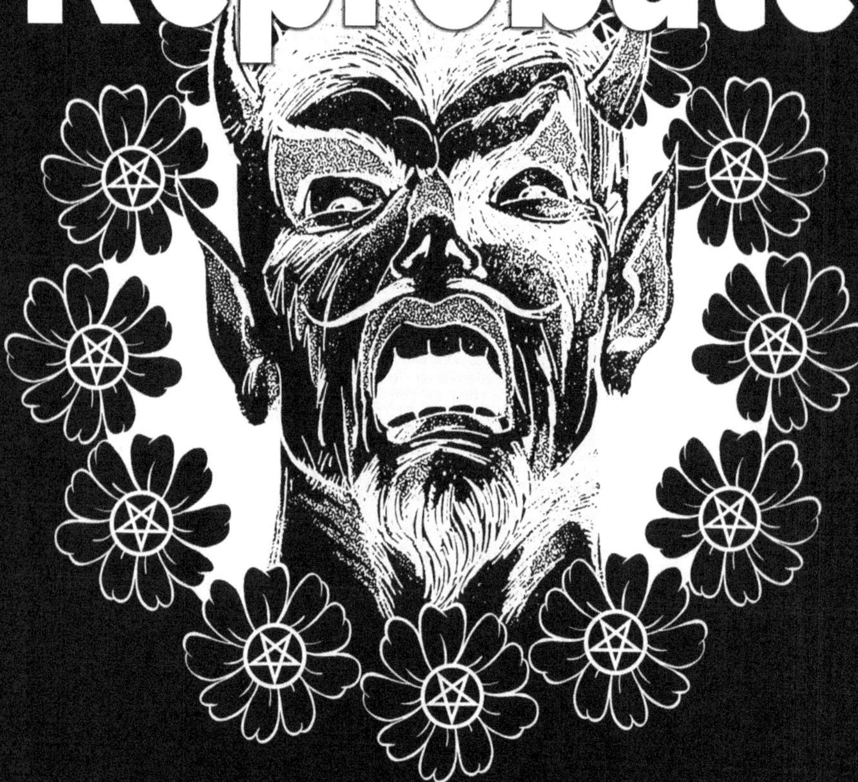

limited edition books, magazines and obscure objects of desire
pop culture archeology, opinionated discussion and more
reprobatepress.com • twitter/instagram: : reprobatepress

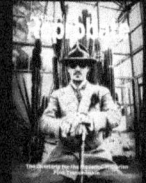 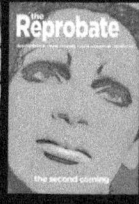 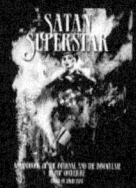 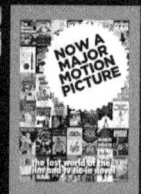 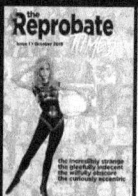 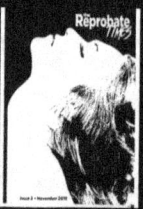

dangerous ideas for dangerous times

www.ingramcontent.com/pod-product-compliance
Lightning Source LLC
Chambersburg PA
CBHW050242220526
45465CB00002B/514